OTHELLO

OTHELLO

William Shakespeare

Edited by
CEDRIC WATTS

WORDSWORTH CLASSICS

First published in 2000 by Wordsworth Editions Limited
8b East Street, Ware, Hertfordshire SG12 9HJ

ISBN 1 85326 018 5

4 6 8 10 9 7 5

Typeset by Antony Gray
Printed and bound in Great Britain by
Mackays of Chatham plc, Chatham, Kent

CONTENTS

General Introduction   7

Introduction   9

Further Reading   23

Note on Shakespeare   25

Acknowledgements and Textual Matters   27

OTHELLO   33

Notes on OTHELLO   133

Glossary   153

GENERAL INTRODUCTION

The Wordsworth Classics' Shakespeare Series, with *Henry V*, *The Merchant of Venice* and *Romeo and Juliet* as its inaugural volumes, presents a newly-edited sequence of William Shakespeare's works. Wordsworth Classics are inexpensive paperbacks for students and for the general reader. Each play in the Shakespeare Series is accompanied by a standard apparatus, including an introduction, explanatory notes and a glossary. The textual editing takes account of recent scholarship while giving the material a careful reappraisal. The apparatus is, however, concise rather than elaborate. We hope that the resultant volumes prove to be handy, reliable and helpful. Above all, we hope that, from Shakespeare's works, readers will derive pleasure, wisdom, provocation, challenges, and insights: insights into his culture and ours, and into the era of civilisation to which his writings have made – and continue to make – such potently influential contributions. Shakespeare's eloquence will, undoubtedly, re-echo 'in states unborn and accents yet unknown'.

CEDRIC WATTS
Series Editor

INTRODUCTION

Othello is one of Shakespeare's greatest tragic dramas: gripping, intense, poignant, harrowing; powerfully eloquent and incisively intelligent. The passage of time has actually increased its cogency. In its treatment of racial prejudice, in its representations of gender and class conflict, and, above all, in its rendering of ascriptions of identity, this play seems vividly contemporary. As has been rightly said:

> Purely as a theatrical experience, *Othello* is as rich and satisfying as only the greatest drama can be. But like all great imaginative work, it speaks to us of our own world, even though it came out of a very different one . . .[M]any of the issues the play raises are relevant, with very slight modification, to our own time. Among the major ones are: The way in which stereotypes are created and come to be accepted (Othello's, Iago's, Desdemona's); women's perception of their own role and men's perception of women; the bases on which people make judgements of others, and the extent to which these are influenced by their own needs and interests; and the nature and limits of one's own responsibility for what happens to oneself. [1]

Of course, the play also has some oddities and puzzles. The earliest texts differ significantly from each other, and they contain some obscurities which continue to perplex editors.[2] Then there are peculiarities in characterisation. For example, the Clown, who appears in Act 3, scenes 1 and 4, is perhaps the least memorable of Shakespeare's comic characters. In stage-production and films, he is usually omitted; and probably few members of the audience regret his absence. Perhaps Shakespeare was kindly providing employment for the company's comedian. Arguably, however, the Clown's fleeting presence as a blithe punster usefully relieves the increasing intensity of the tragic action. The play's dramatic rhythm consists of alternations of reflection and violence, argument and uproar, conversation and emotional eruptions; and the Clown's wisecracks about wind instruments and lying form part of the pattern of contrasts, offsetting the sinister exploitation of ambiguous terms ('honest', 'nature', and again 'lying') by Iago.

As for Iago himself: his motives have long been a puzzle for commentators. Coleridge famously claimed that, in him, we see 'the motive-hunting of motiveless malignity'.[3] Commentators who take a relatively sympathetic view of Othello tend to emphasise the destructive brilliance of Iago, whereas commentators who take a relatively critical view of Othello tend to play down Iago's importance. In *Shakespearean Tragedy* (1904), A. C. Bradley devoted many pages to an elaborate and perceptive analysis of Iago's character, declaring him 'supreme among Shakespeare's evil characters'; but in *The Common Pursuit* (1952), F. R. Leavis remarked dismissively that Iago is 'merely ancillary': 'not much more than a necessary piece of dramatic mechanism' – something needed to help the plot along.[4] In fact, Iago is a layered characterisation of the kind to be scanned in different ways. Considered as a realistic creation, he can be seen to have implicit motivation underlying his mixture of explicit, avowed motives.[5] One of those implicit motives is the desire to vindicate a cynicism antagonised by virtue; another is to fulfil an intelligence which delights in destructively paradoxical transformations of the people around him, a power-seeking which over-compensates for his low rank. It is Iago's more protean jealousy which generates Othello's localised jealousy. Another way of scanning Iago is to see him as a sophisticated development of the ingratiating stage villain, the Machiavellian rogue who (like Barabas in Marlowe's *Jew of Malta* or Richard in Shakespeare's *Richard III*) takes us into his confidence and erodes normal ethical responses by making us his accomplices. When he asks, 'And what's he then, that says I play the villain?', he is clearly addressing the audience; and at that point realism modulates into a very traditional surrealism – the surrealism generated when the fictional world openly colludes with the non-fictional.[6]

Iago (as Bradley observed) has intermittent resemblances to his creator, Shakespeare. When Iago says of his scheme, ' 'Tis here,

but yet confused', and when he reflects that whether Cassio or
Roderigo dies, 'every way makes my gain', we sense similarities to
the authorial mixture of calculation and opportunistic improvisa-
tion which a study of textual variations and of Shakespeare's
plotting reveals. In the case of *Othello*, the most notorious oddity of
the plot is the 'double time-scheme', which was noted as long ago
as 1692 by Thomas Rymer in his *Short View of Tragedy*.[7] The gist of
this matter is as follows. Iago persuades Othello that, since his
marriage to Desdemona, she has committed adultery with Cassio –
not once but on numerous occasions. Various 'long-time' references give the impression that an ample period has elapsed for this
purpose. On the other hand, close attention to the unfolding
events makes evident the fact that only thirty-three hours or so
elapse between the arrival of Desdemona on Cyprus and her
eventual death at Othello's hands. On the first night, she is in bed
with Othello, and their privacy is disrupted by Cassio's drunken
brawl; on the second night, she dies. There simply has not been
time for the alleged repeated adultery to occur. As Rymer puts it:

> The *Audience* must suppose a great many bouts [i.e. adulterous
> encounters], to make the plot operate. They must deny their
> senses, to reconcile it to common sense: or make it any way
> consistent, and hang together.[8]

Thus the plot founders on gross illogicality; or would so founder,
if we maintained a precise chronological awareness. As has been
often remarked, however, audiences are generally untroubled by
the illogicality: being so caught up in the moment-by-moment
development of the accelerating drama, the spectators reconcile
imaginatively the logically irreconcilable. Subliminally, this may
add to our sympathy with Othello: for, as he is fooled by Iago's
manipulation of evidence, so we are fooled by Shakespeare's.
(Shakespeare was a maestro of the double time-scheme: he uses it
in *Love's Labour's Lost*, *Richard II*, *The Merchant of Venice* and
Measure for Measure, for example.)
     Anyone who doubts Shakespeare's creative and transformative
genius need only look at the source-tale for *Othello*, Giraldi
Cinthio's story (in *Gli Hecatommithi*, 1565) of a Moorish captain and
'Disdemona', his bride. Cinthio's narrative is straggling and epi-
sodic; Shakespeare has compressed and co-ordinated the material,

breathing radiant life into drab clay. Cinthio offers a sordid crime-
story; Shakespeare has created an eloquent and intense tragedy.
When Shakespeare's vengeful Moor advances on his sleeping wife,
musing 'It is the cause, it is the cause, my soul', he attempts to
convert a murder into an act of justice, and his will poignantly
flinches before her serene beauty. In Cinthio, we find a contrast-
ingly sordid situation. There, the Moor conceals his accomplice,
the Ensign (who is armed with a sand-filled stocking), in a closet
opening on the bedchamber. He orders his wife out of bed to
ascertain the cause of a sound there.

> The unfortunate Disdemona got out of bed, and as soon as she
> was near the closet, the Ensign came out and, being strong and
> muscular, he gave her a frightful blow in the small of her back,
> which made the Lady fall down at once, scarcely able to draw
> her breath. With the little voice she had she called on the Moor
> to help her. But he, jumping out of bed, said to her, 'You
> wicked woman, you are having the reward of your infidelity.
> This is how women are treated who, pretending to love their
> husbands, put horns on their heads.' [9]

She calls on God to witness her fidelity and to help her; but to no
avail, as the Ensign continues to bludgeon her to death. The
Ensign and the Moor then pull the ceiling down on her, so that
she seems to be the victim of an unlucky accident; and for a while
their ruse is successful. The Moor's death occurs long afterwards
(as a result of further intrigues by the Ensign): 'he was finally slain
by Disdemona's relatives, as he richly deserved'. Still later, the
Ensign, having hatched a different plot, is tested by torture and
subsequently dies 'miserably' at his home.

Where the Moor is concerned, Cinthio's narrative carries a
partly-racist warning which is voiced by Disdemona: 'Italian ladies
will learn by my example not to tie themselves to a man whom
Nature, Heaven, and manner of life separate from us.'[10] G. K.
Hunter comments on Elizabethan attitudes:

> They had, to start with, the basic common man's attitude that all
> foreigners are curious and inferior – the more curious the more
> inferior, in the sense of the proverb quoted by Purchas: 'Three
> Moors to a Portuguese; three Portuguese to an Englishman.'

They had also the basic and ancient sense that black is the colour of sin and death, 'the badge of hell, The hue of dungeons, and the Schoole of night' (as Shakespeare himself says). This supposition is found all over the world . . . from the earliest to the latest times; and in the West there is a continuous and documented tradition of it. [11]

Devils were often depicted or described as black-faced; paintings of the scourging of Christ sometimes included a black scourger; and, in folk-drama, St George's enemy is termed 'Black Morocco Dog' and 'Black Prince of Darkness'. Aaron, the villain of Shakespeare's first tragedy, *Titus Andronicus*, is a 'coal-black' Moor who delights in adultery, rape, mutilation and murder: 'Aaron will have his soul black like his face', he gleefully declares.[12] Even in *The Merchant of Venice*, in which Portia assures the Prince of Morocco that she has no prejudice against his skin-colour, she privately declares:

If he have the condition of a saint, and the complexion of a devil, I had rather he should shrive me than wive me.[13]

In 1601, Queen Elizabeth proclaimed her discontent at 'the great number of "negars and blackamoores" which are crept into the realm . . . to the annoyance of her own people', these aliens being 'mostly infidels' who consume 'relief '; and she appointed Caspar van Zeuden, a merchant, to deport them. [14]

Against this background, Shakespeare's depiction of Othello offers a remarkably thorough subversion of racial prejudice. From the very start of the play, such prejudice is being evoked: Iago and Roderigo yell to Brabantio that his daughter is being 'tupped' by 'an old black ram', by 'the devil', 'a Barbary horse', 'a lascivious Moor', an 'extravagant and wheeling stranger'. Later, the horrified Brabantio declares it so unnatural for Desdemona to seek 'the sooty bosom of such a thing' that Othello must have used black magic, witchcraft, 'practices of cunning hell'. In the opening scenes, then, a familiar gamut of prejudicial attitudes is being evoked: the black man is a suspicious outsider, an immigrant guilty of evil practices, a devil or an associate of devils, and a beast driven by lust; so that his union with a young white woman must be hideously unnatural. In utter contrast, we are shown, and hear, Othello himself. He is more civilised than the white representatives of European civilisation around him: poised, even majestic (for he is of royal line), cool, steady, doughty, equable, rational, fair-minded; the general whom the Venetian empire trusts for its safety.[15] When all around him are ready for a battle in the streets, he responds: 'Keep up your bright swords, for the dew will rust them.' In response to racist provocation, he remains unruffled. His address to the Signiory is a compellingly authoritative and persuasive feat of reasoned rhetoric. In response to the charge that he used black magic, he calls in Desdemona to speak, and she testifies with moving lucidity:

> I saw Othello's visage in his mind,
> And to his honours and his valiant parts
> Did I my soul and fortunes consecrate.

As for the notion that he may be lust-driven, he protests (probably too much) that he is not governed by 'the palate of . . . appetite', the 'young affects' being in him 'defunct'. In short, the love of Othello and Desdemona is established as a superb triumph of mutuality over the cruel, barbaric and sexually-obsessed forces of racial prejudice.

Shakespeare was fascinated by the figure of the charismatic but vulnerable martial hero: the man of courage, hardihood and prowess who may prove impetuous rather than prudent; the glamorous, larger-than-life figure who is manipulable by the crafty. A famous example is Harry Hotspur, honour-driven, who can be manipulated by Worcester and Northumberland; another is Antony, 'triple pillar of the world', out-manoeuvred by Octavius; and yet another is Coriolanus, doughty on the battle-field, inept in the world of politics. Othello is, arguably, the most attractive and impressive of this line of martial figures. What, then, of his downfall, and of his hideous murder of Desdemona? F. R. Leavis claimed that the seeds of disaster lay far less in Iago's machinations than in Othello's egotism. Othello, this critic argued, has 'a habit of self-approving self-dramatisation': he is blinkered by concern for his own reputation; and if (as Bradley had said) his trust, where he trusts, is absolute, it must be invested in the fellow-soldier, Iago, rather than in his own wife. Certainly, that preoccupation with reputation and self-image is a recurrent characteristic, from his address for the Signiory to the final speech before his suicide. But

Leavis did not make sufficient allowance for what Othello's blackness constantly suggests: namely, the cultural insecurity of someone who is subject to explicit prejudice; the understandable insecurity of one who comes from an exotic background, has become a Christian and a redoubtable servant of a European city-state, but whose otherness is conspicuous, and whose eminence and marriage may engender vicious hostility.[16] It is that insecurity which Iago ruthlessly exploits, most craftily when he suggests that Desdemona's very transcendence of racial prejudice may be construed as treachery — treachery to family, country, race and the conventional world of prejudice; so that betrayal of her husband would be consistent with a deep-seated perfidious tendency. After all, had not Brabantio said: 'Look to her, Moor, if thou hast eyes to see: / She has deceived her father, and may thee'? That insecurity is symbolically resolved in the manner of Othello's death.

> . . . And say besides, that in Aleppo once,
> Where a malignant and a turbaned Turk
> Beat a Venetian and traduced the state,
> I took by th'throat the circumcisèd dog,
> And smote him — thus!

The stabbing of the imagined enemy of the Venetian state becomes the stabbing of the defender of the state. The image of the exotic foe, and the contrasting image of the defender of European civilisation, suddenly merge. Aggressor and defender, Muslim and Christian, 'barbarian' and Venetian, fuse in death, impaled on one blade.

In their love, Othello and Desdemona seemed to have transcended racial and sexual stereotyping, the imposition of reductive notions upon reality. But the stereotypical habit of mind helps to ensnare them; and that habit insidiously re-appears. Consider the speech I have just quoted. The Turk (in Aleppo, a Syrian city within the Turkish empire) may have beaten a Venetian and 'traduced the state', but did he deserve death? We are told he is 'a malignant . . . Turk': is he malignant and a Turk, or deemed malignant *because* he is a Turk? What's so wrong about wearing a turban, a sign of faith like a cross on a Christian's neck-chain? Again, if he is 'circumcisèd' (circumcision being a religious rite for Muslims), what's so bad about that? And, last in the sequence of pejoratives, this human being is referred to as a 'dog': so Othello himself upholds that system of demeaning stereotyping (depicting human beings as less than human, merely as animals) of which he – formerly termed 'ram' and 'Barbary horse' – had been a victim. After Othello's death, the supposedly civilised Christians will subject Iago, that 'damnèd slave', 'dog', 'demi-devil' and 'hellish villain', to barbaric tortures: 'any cunning cruelty / That can torment him much and hold him long'. Once Othello, saying 'Keep up your bright swords, for the dew will rust them', had seemed urbanely superior to the notion that differences should be resolved by a prompt recourse to violence; but that primitive 'virile' notion ensnares him and others, and destroys Desdemona.

As for Desdemona: who knows her best? Not her own father, who is incredulous on learning that she has eloped with the Moor. Not Othello, whose personal insecurity leads him to trust Iago rather than her. It may be tempting to propose Emilia, that fore-runner of feminists. Emilia tries to console and sustain Desdemona after Othello becomes jealous and violent; and it is she who advocates equality of desire between men and women.

> Let husbands know
> Their wives have sense like them: they see, and smell,
> And have their palates both for sweet and sour,
> As husbands have. What is it that they do,
> When they change us for others? Is it sport?
> I think it is. And doth affection breed it?
> I think it doth. Is't frailty that thus errs?
> It is so too. And have not we affections,
> Desires for sport, and frailty, as men have?
> Then let them use us well; else let them know,
> The ills we do, their ills instruct us so.

It's a strikingly radical speech at this juncture in a drama which has repeatedly displayed patriarchal dominance. In its postulation of equivalence in affections, desires and fallibility between men and women, Emilia's argument seems positive and progressive. Its tone is not quiet, intimate and conversational; markedly towards the end, the tone is that of public address: one can imagine the speaker turning in admonition to the men in the audience. As a defence of people who are the uncomprehended victims of stereotyping, it ranks with Shylock's famous vindication (the speech beginning

'Hath not a Jew eyes?') in *The Merchant of Venice*.[17] Like his speech,
however, Emilia's has a destructive ending. Shylock concludes that
since Christians are vengeful, he is entitled to use vengeance
himself. Emilia concludes that since men are unfaithful, women are
entitled to be unfaithful in turn. Desdemona's response marks a
clear difference:

> Good night, good night. God me such usage send:
> Not to pick bad from bad, but by bad mend!

In other words, two wrongs don't make one right: rather than
imitate bad examples, one should learn to behave better. It's a simple
sententious couplet but (in this play) refreshingly sound morality.

The element of cynicism in Emilia's response makes one see
how she may have been a suitable partner for Iago (who declares
that love is basically a matter of lust); and though she eventually
betrays her husband's machinations, she does so too late, after
furthering them by stealing – and long failing to admit the theft
of – the fatal handkerchief. Thomas Rymer derided the significance of that item of fine linen:

> Had it been *Desdemona*'s Garter, the Sagacious Moor might
> have smelt a Rat: but the Handkerchief is so remote a trifle, no
> Booby, on this side *Mauritania*, cou'd make any consequence
> from it.[18]

What Rymer missed is the symbolic investment in that handkerchief. Othello's narrative about it (whether true or false),[19] invests
it with immense cultural significance: the handkerchief signifies
the cultural difference and ancestral heritage which have been
entrusted to Desdemona.

Here, as so often in *Othello*, a character says, in effect, 'Don't be
deceived by appearances: the reality may be quite different.'
Desdemona and the Duke say this in reference to Othello himself;
Brabantio and, crucially, Iago say it of Desdemona. The trust
which others repose in 'honest' Iago is exploited by him to destroy
trust in others; and one of his weapons is stereotyping – the
imposition of reductively simple models on complex actualities.
He invites it and wields it. He himself is stereotyped as 'honest': as
the kind of tough comrade-in-arms who has a gritty common
sense (and who may be taken, condescendingly, for granted).

Desdemona has defied the stereotyping of women as submissive:
she has done so by her courageous independence of attitude. In
addition, she has defied the stereotyping of black men as devilish:
she has done so by her readiness to love the noble Othello. But
Iago persuades Othello that she has reverted to stereotype in
hankering after a white lover, a young European. Her spirited
defence of the demoted Cassio can then be construed not as
generous loyalty to a friend but as cynical support of her lover.
Othello, having regarded her as his 'soul's joy', his courageous
partner in marital love, is now seduced by Iago's insinuations, and
melodramatically identifies her with the stereotype of the whore,
the promiscuous adulteress. Instead of weighing diverse evidence
judiciously (as the Signiory had done), he escapes inner division by
adopting the stereotype of the decisive man of action who
proceeds promptly to violence. After all, he has no reason to doubt
the integrity of Iago, his long-standing comrade-in-arms; Othello
knows the battlefield better than the character of Venetian women;
and his hearsay knowledge of women is arrogantly stereotypical:

> O curse of marriage,
> That we can call these delicate creatures ours,
> And not their appetites! I had rather be a toad,
> And live upon the vapour of a dungeon,
> Than keep a corner in the thing I love
> For others' uses. Yet, 'tis the plague of great ones;
> Prerogatived are they less than the base;
> 'Tis destiny unshunnable, like death:
> Even then this forkèd plague is fated to us
> When we do quicken.

Simple patterns thus reduce and falsify the complex reality. Wives
have uncontrollable sexual appetites; great men are, in this respect,
more vulnerable than commoners; and to marry an adulteress is an
inescapable destiny for eminent men – they are born to it. The
'honourable' – or crazily patriarchal – punishment for such adultery
is reflexively assumed to be murder. *Othello* could thus be summed
up as a study of the tragic consequences of stereotyping.

Such a summary would, however, itself veer too much towards
a simplifying stereotype. When we respond to a good stage-
production, we are caught up in the unfolding drama with its

tensions and cruel ironies, and the range of diverse eloquence reverberates; the sensuous imagination stirs. Edward Said once offered an anti-theoretical literary theory:

> [I]t is the critic's job to provide resistances to theory, to open it up toward historical reality, toward society, toward human needs and interests . . . [20]

The *critic's* job? *Othello* shows that this has long been the creative writer's job. 'Resistances to theory'? Theories of human nature, whether expressed within the play or outside it, here meet the resistance of a complex, resonantly articulate and moving reflection of 'historical reality, . . . society, . . . human needs and interests'. The operations of jealousy and prejudice (which we all know, all too well) are given multiple and epitomising enactment. Our moral judgements are challenged by the appeals of the aesthetic; our analyses are ambushed by the seductions of the senses. Iago gloats over the fallen Othello, declaring:

> Not poppy, nor mandragora,
> Nor all the drowsy syrups of the world,
> Shall ever medicine thee to that sweet sleep
> Which thou owedst yesterday.

And as he does so, our moral disapproval of his attitude is beguiled by the seductive rhetoric: 'Not poppy, nor mandragora', 'drowsy syrups of the world': even before the sense is fully grasped, the phrasing sings in the ears and offers shimmery images to the mind's eye. Again, consider the rhetoric as Othello, at the bedside, prepares to murder Desdemona:

> Put out the light, and then put out the light.
> If I quench thee, thou flaming minister,
> I can again thy former light restore
> Should I repent me; but once put out thy light,
> Thou cunning'st pattern of excelling nature,
> I know not where is that Promethean heat
> That can thy light relume. When I have plucked the rose,
> I cannot give it vital growth again:
> It needs must wither. I'll smell it on the tree.
> O balmy breath, that dost almost persuade
> Justice to break her sword!

Here, our moral dismay at the act is blended with sensuous pleasure at the euphoniously eloquent rhetoric in its alliteratively rhythmic fluency, and perhaps also with aesthetic pleasure at the elegant deployment of the cruel irony in those last lines. If Othello had only allowed himself to be fully governed by his sensuous delight in that 'balmy breath', he would have broken the sword not of justice but of his own lethal folly.

Appealing in such ways to our minds and imaginations, to our critical faculties and to our senses, this tragedy, in all its emotional and linguistic range, remains powerfully cogent today.

NOTES TO THE INTRODUCTION

1 Fenella and Gāmini Salgādo: *Shakespeare: 'Othello'* (London: Penguin, 1985), pp. 88–9.
2 For example, some editors suspect corruption at 1.3.263–4 and 4.2.63–5; and much-debated cruces include 'ice-brook's temper' at 5.2.253 and 'the base Indian/Judean' at 5.2.346. (References are to this edition.).
3 S. T. Coleridge: *Shakespearean Criticism*, ed. T. M. Raysor (2 vols.; London: Dent, 1960), Vol. 1, p. 44. Other editions give: 'the motive-hunting of a motiveless malignity'.
4 A. C. Bradley: *Shakespearean Tragedy* [1904] (London: Macmillan, 1957), pp. 169–94. F. R. Leavis: *The Common Pursuit* [1952] (Harmondsworth: Penguin, 1962), p. 138.
5 Iago's avowed motives include: thwarted ambition; revenge for Othello's supposed adultery with Emilia; lust for Desdemona; Cassio's supposed adultery with Emilia; and hatred of Cassio's 'daily beauty'.
6 Pantomimes attune us to such illogical but gratifying shifts in convention – as when fictional characters, on stage, seek help from children in the audience. So do musicals and operas: for example, when the fictional action is repeatedly interrupted by the patrons' applause. Of course, in pantomimes, musicals and operas, characters readily shift from dialogue to song. One obvious 'operatic' feature of Shakespearian drama is the alternation of prose with verse: some of Othello's speeches resemble arias in their isolable splendour.
7 Thomas Rymer: *A Short View of Tragedy* (London: Richard Baldwin, dated '1693' but issued in 1692), pp. 115, 121, 123, 125–7, 132. The 'discovery' of the double time-scheme has sometimes been attributed to John Wilson (alias 'Christopher North') in his articles for *Blackwood's Edinburgh Magazine* in 1850, but Rymer first expounded the problem. (The Wilson discussion is in Vol. 67, April and May 1850, pp. 489–512 and 626–34.)

8 *A Short View of Tragedy*, p. 123. Desdemona lands on Cyprus around 4
   p.m. on Saturday and dies on Sunday night. 'Long time' references
   include these: Othello is persuaded that Desdemona and Cassio have
   committed adultery '[a] thousand times' (and in Othello's marital bed:
   4.1.139, 4.1.201–2); Emilia says that Iago asked her 'a hundred times' to
   steal the handkerchief; and Bianca complains that Cassio has neglected
   her for a week. The charge against Desdemona is clearly that of adultery,
   not of pre-marital intercourse with Cassio; and, during the voyage, she
   and he are in different ships.

9 *Narrative and Dramatic Sources of Shakespeare*, Vol. 7, ed. Geoffrey
   Bullough (London: Routledge and Kegan Paul; New York: Columbia
   University Press; 1973), pp. 250–51.

10 *Narrative and Dramatic Sources of Shakespeare*, Vol. 7, p. 248.

11 G. K. Hunter: 'Othello and Colour Prejudice' in *Proceedings of the British
   Academy*, 53 (London: Oxford University Press, 1968), pp. 140–41. The
   Ndembu people of Africa associate blackness with 'badness or evil . . . ,
   witchcraft/sorcery . . . , death [and] sexual desire', according to V. W.
   Turner's 'Colour Classification in Ndembu Ritual' in *Anthropological
   Approaches to the Study of Religion*, ed. Michael Banton (London:
   Tavistock, 1966), pp. 60–61.

12 *Titus Andronicus*, ed. J. C. Maxwell (London: Methuen, 1961), 3.1.205.
   Aaron describes himself and his son as 'coal-black'; he has a 'fleece of
   woolly hair', and he calls his son 'thick-lipped'. Henry Peachum's
   drawing of a 16th-century production of *Titus Andronicus* shows a very
   black Aaron. This increases the probability that Othello, another Moor,
   should be regarded as black-skinned; and he refers to his own face as
   'begrimed and black'. Contemporaneous pictures of Moors depict them
   as both Arabian and sub-Saharan African in appearance: see *The Norton
   Shakespeare* (New York and London: Norton, 1997), p. 2092. John Leo's
   geographical and historical survey of Africa (1550) says that while some
   Moors are 'white or tawny', others are 'black'.

13 *The Merchant of Venice*, ed. Cedric Watts (London: Wordsworth, 2000),
   1.2.120–22. Although a stage-direction in the earliest texts describes the
   Prince of Morocco as 'tawny', his and Portia's speeches imply a darker
   complexion.

14 *Historical Manuscripts Commission. Calendar of the Manuscripts of the Most
   Hon. The Marquis of Salisbury*, Pt. 11 (London: His Majesty's Stationery
   Office, 1906), p. 569. This differs from the version in *Tudor Royal
   Proclamations*, Vol. 3, ed. P. L. Hughes and J. F. Larkin (New Haven and
   London: Yale University Press, 1969), pp. 221–2.

15 One source of Othello's character was the historic John Leo (Leo
   Africanus), whose *A Geographical Historie of Africa* was published in John
   Pory's English translation in 1600. Leo, according to his own and Pory's
   accounts, was a well-educated Moor of noble family who travelled

widely in exotic regions, fought in wars, served the King of Fez, was captured by pirates, and at Rome was entertained hospitably by Pope Leo X. There, having originally been a Muslim, he became a Christian. Pory says that he was a great orator and scholar.

16 Paul Robeson, the black singer and actor who played Othello, remarked: 'But the color is essentially secondary – except as it emphasizes the difference in *culture*. This is the important thing.' (Quoted in Marvin Rosenberg's *The Masks of Othello*: Berkeley and Los Angeles: University of California Press, 1961; p. 195.)

17 *The Merchant of Venice*, 3.1.52–66. Shylock, though speaking in prose, employs a similar catechismic question-and-answer format.

18 *A Short View of Tragedy*, p. 140. (The page-numbering is irregular: p. 140 follows immediately after p. 135.)

19 See 'Othello's Magical Handkerchief ' in John Sutherland and Cedric Watts: *Henry V, War Criminal? and Other Shakespeare Puzzles* (Oxford: Oxford University Press, 2000), pp. 76–84.

20 Edward Said: *The World, the Text, and the Critic* (London: Faber and Faber, 1984), p. 242.

FURTHER READING
(in chronological order)

A. C. Bradley: *Shakespearean Tragedy* [1904]. Basingstoke: Macmillan, 1992.

G. Wilson Knight: 'The Othello Music' in *The Wheel of Fire* [1930]. London: Methuen, 1986.

F. R. Leavis: 'Diabolic Intellect and the Noble Hero: or The Sentimentalist's Othello' in *The Common Pursuit*. London: Chatto & Windus, 1952.

Robert B. Heilman: *Magic in the Web: Action and Language in 'Othello'*. Lexington: University of Kentucky Press, 1956.

John Holloway: *The Story of the Night: Studies in Shakespeare's Major Tragedies*. London: Routledge and Kegan Paul, 1961.

Marvin Rosenberg: *The Masks of Othello*. Berkeley and Los Angeles: University of California Press, 1961.

Eldred Jones: *Othello's Countrymen: The African in English Renaissance Drama*. London: Oxford University Press, 1965.

Shakespeare: 'Othello': A Casebook, ed. John Wain. London and Basingstoke: Macmillan, 1971.

Narrative and Dramatic Sources of Shakespeare, Vol. 7, ed. Geoffrey Bullough. London: Routledge and Kegan Paul; New York: Columbia University Press, 1973.

Leslie A. Fiedler: *The Stranger in Shakespeare*. London: Croom Helm, 1973.

Samuel Schoenbaum: *William Shakespeare: A Compact Documentary Life*. London and New York: Oxford University Press, 1977, rpt. 1987.

Jane Adamson: *'Othello' as Tragedy: Some Problems of Judgment and Feeling*. Cambridge: Cambridge University Press, 1980.

Martin L. Wine: *Othello: Text and Performance*. Basingstoke and London: Macmillan, 1984.

Fenella and Gāmini Salgādo: *Shakespeare: 'Othello'*. London: Penguin, 1985.

The Cambridge Companion to Shakespeare Studies, ed. Stanley Wells. Cambridge: Cambridge University Press, 1986.

Julie Hankey: *Plays in Performance: 'Othello': William Shakespeare*. Bristol: Bristol Classical Press, 1987.

Martin Elliott: *Shakespeare's Invention of Othello: A Study in Early Modern English*. Basingstoke and London: Macmillan, 1988.

Longman Critical Essays: Othello, ed. Linda Cookson and Bryan Loughrey. Harlow: Longman, 1991.

Brian Vickers: *Appropriating Shakespeare: Contemporary Critical Quarrels*. New Haven and London: Yale University Press, 1993.

Graham Bradshaw: *Misrepresentations: Shakespeare and the Materialists*. Ithaca, N.Y.: Cornell University Press, 1993.

Virginia Mason Vaughan: *Othello: A Contextual History*. Cambridge: Cambridge University Press, 1994.

Russ McDonald: *The Bedford Companion to Shakespeare*. New York: St Martin's Press; Basingstoke: Macmillan; 1996.

E. A. J. Honigmann: *The Texts of 'Othello' and Shakespearian Revision*. London and New York: Routledge, 1996.

E. A. J. Honigmann: 'Introduction': *Othello*. Walton-on-Thames: Nelson, 1997.

Kenneth S. Rothwell: *Shakespeare on Screen: A Century of Film and Television*. Cambridge: Cambridge University Press, 1999.

John Sutherland and Cedric Watts: *Henry V, War Criminal? and Other Shakespeare Puzzles*. Oxford: Oxford University Press, 2000.

NOTE ON SHAKESPEARE

Details of Shakespeare's early life are scanty. He was the son of a prosperous merchant of Stratford-upon-Avon, and tradition gives his date of birth as 23 April, 1564; certainly, three days later, he was christened at the parish church. It is likely that he attended the local Grammar School but had no university education. Of his early career there is no record, though John Aubrey states that he was a country schoolmaster. In 1582 Shakespeare married Anne Hathaway, with whom he had two daughters, Susanna and Judith, and a son, Hamnet, who died in 1596. How he became involved with the stage in London is uncertain, but he was sufficiently established as a playwright by 1592 to be criticised in print as a challengingly versatile 'upstart Crow'. He was a leading member of the Lord Chamberlain's company, which became the King's Men on the accession of James I in 1603. Being not only a playwright and actor but also a 'sharer' (one of the owners of the company, entitled to a share of the profits), Shakespeare prospered greatly, as is proven by the numerous records of his financial transactions. Towards the end of his life, he loosened his ties with London and retired to New Place, the large property in Stratford which he had bought in 1597. He died on 23 April, 1616, and is buried in the place of his baptism, Holy Trinity Church. The earliest collected edition of his plays, the First Folio, was published in 1623, and its prefatory verse-tributes include Ben Jonson's famous declaration, 'He was not of an age, but for all time'.

ACKNOWLEDGEMENTS AND TEXTUAL MATTERS

With a title like that, this section may seem skippable; but the textual comments could be useful if you have to write an essay on *Othello*, or if you face an examination-question about it, or if you are involved in a production of the play. The gist of the matter is that, from Shakespeare's day to the present, the text has been significantly and fruitfully variable, and it will long remain so.

I have consulted, and am indebted to, numerous editions of *Othello*, notably those by: Horace Howard Furness (1886; reprinted, New York: Dover, 1963); Alice Walker and John Dover Wilson (London: Cambridge University Press, 1957); M. R. Ridley (the Arden Shakespeare: London, Methuen, 1958); Norman Sanders (Cambridge: Cambridge University Press, 1984); Stanley Wells and Gary Taylor (Oxford: Oxford University Press, 1988); Andrew Murphy (Hemel Hempstead: Prentice Hall and Harvester Wheatsheaf, 1995); Stephen Greenblatt *et al.* (New York and London: Norton, 1997); and E. A. J. Honigmann (the Arden Shakespeare: Walton-on-Thames: Thomas Nelson & Sons, 1997, rpt. 1998). I am grateful for the advice of Prof. Mario Curreli and Mr J. M. Glauser.

Othello was probably written between 1601 and 1604, and it was performed at Whitehall on 1 November 1604. The first printed text, the First Quarto (Q1), appeared in 1622, six years after Shakespeare's death. Next, the play was included in the First Folio of 1623 (F1), the first 'Collected Edition' of Shakespeare's works.[1] This volume was prepared by two of Shakespeare's colleagues, John Heminges and Henry Condell.

The Q1 and F1 texts of *Othello* are substantially similar, but they frequently differ significantly from each other.

F1, for example, contains some 160 lines not present in Q1,
including some extended passages — the longest running to 22
lines. Q1 also contains a number of lines and phrases which do
not appear in F1 and includes more than fifty oaths which are
not present in F1. The stage directions also vary considerably
between Q1 and F1 and there are over a thousand other minor
variations between the two texts.[2]

Some of the differences are explained by early cutting: F1 includes
some passages which appear to have been cut from the script
(perhaps to reduce performance-time) before it was set in type as
Q1. In other cases, censorship operated: the 1606 'Acte to Restraine
Abuses of Players' threatened with a fine of £10 any actor profanely
uttering the name of God, Christ, the Holy Ghost or the Trinity;
and there are clear signs that this affected the later text but not the
earlier.[3] Q1 contains some interesting material which is lacking in
F1, and F1 contains a larger quantity of interesting material which is
absent from Q1. Usually, editors endeavour to achieve what they
deem to be the best compromise between these two early versions,
so that a conflated text results; they supply conjectural readings on
those occasions when the phrasing seems incorrect or obscure; and
they adopt modern conventions of spelling, punctuation and
presentation. This Wordsworth edition, similarly, offers a conflated
text; and the annotations draw attention to particularly interesting
variations between Q1 and F1, while providing illustrations of the
differences between early and current conventions. Anyone who is
interested in seeing the originals, 'warts and all', may consult
facsimile reprints.[4]

One large difference between Q1 and F1 is that only in the latter
does Desdemona sing the 'Willow Song'. It appears to have been
cut from the version which was printed as Q1. Perhaps the boy
actor who played Desdemona found that his voice was breaking;
perhaps the part was taken over by a boy who proved to be
inadequate as a singer; or perhaps the company simply needed to
shorten the play. Loss of the song is, however, loss of a poignantly
intimate interlude between the scene in which Desdemona has
been subjected to abusive violence by Othello and the scene in
which, after the attack on Cassio, Desdemona will be murdered.
Furthermore, the lyrics comment ironically on the tragic action. In

them, the forlorn woman says of her apparently faithless lover, 'Let nobody blame him; his scorn I approve': an anticipation of Desdemona's desperately loyal attempt, in her dying moments, to deflect blame from Othello.

Another significant difference occurs as Othello attempts to kill her. Q1 offers this:

Des.	But halfe an houre, but while I say one prayer.
Oth.	Tis too late. *he stifles her.*
Des.	O Lord, Lord, Lord. Emillia *calls within.*
Em.	My Lord, my Lord, what ho, my Lord, my Lord.
Oth.	What voyce is this? not dead? not yet quite dead?
	I that am cruell, am yet mercifull,
	I would not haue thee linger in thy pain, —so, so.

F1, on the other hand, offers this:

Des.	But halfe an houre.
Oth.	Being done, there is no pawse.
Des.	But while I say one prayer.
Oth.	It is too late. *Smothers her.*
	Æmilia at the doore.
Æmil.	My Lord, my Lord? What hoa?
	My Lord, my Lord.
Oth.	What noise is this? Not dead? not yet quite dead?
	I that am cruell, am yet mercifull,
	I would not haue thee linger in thy paine?
	So, so.

Desdemona's 'O Lord, Lord, Lord' appears in one text but not the other. If a director of the play chooses to include this invocation, there are further choices to be made. Perhaps the words '*he stifles her*' appear half a line early: after all, some of the other stage-directions are incorrectly located. In that case, the invocation could be re-located and uttered just *before* Othello starts to stifle her. She has begged for the opportunity to pray, and this could be her distraught commencement of a prayer to the Lord God, an attempt truncated as she is stifled. On the other hand, the director might remain faithful to the arrangement in Q1. In this case, when Othello ceases the act of stifling and thinks she is dead, Desdemona partly recovers and uncannily calls out, her voice from the bed being eerily echoed by the 'My Lord, my Lord' from Emilia outside: a discordant conjunction of the Lord God and Lord Othello. Hence Othello's confused response ('What voyce is this?') before his recognition that Desdemona yet lives. F1's version, in which 'What noise is this?' refers to Emilia's cries outside the door, eliminates the echo, is easier to stage, and is preferred (as less jarring) by some critics; but it is arguably less striking and complex.

Numerous other instances of interesting contrasts could be adduced. For instance: appearing in F1 but absent from Q1 are Othello's superbly eloquent comparison of his vengeful thoughts to the Pontic Sea (in this edition, Act 3, scene 3, lines 456-63), Desdemona's moving asseveration of her innocence (Act 4, scene 2, lines 153-66), and Emilia's 'feminist' speech (Act 4, scene 3, lines 86-103).

In short, there is more 'play' – flexibility, variability and adaptability – in *Othello* than you might at first imagine. If you compare a couple of modern texts with each other, and compare either of them with the Q1 and F1 versions, you soon realise that the options for readers, critics, actors and directors are admirably numerous. My annotations indicate a range of those options. One reason for Shakespeare's durability is that the divergences, ambiguities and puzzles in the early texts provide plenty of room for later variations, adaptations and interpretations. The script of this tragedy was evidently changing in response to diverse needs and pressures even before it was first captured for the printed page – after which it could repeatedly be transformed in the imaginations of readers and audiences.

I hope that the present edition of *Othello* represents a useful compromise between the early texts, Shakespeare's intentions (insofar as they can be reasonably inferred) and modern requirements. The glossary explains unfamiliar terms, and the annotations offer clarification of obscurities. In any case, as you read the play, you may find that you are editing it to suit yourself, even as you are staging it in the boundless theatre of your imagination.

NOTES TO THIS SECTION

1 Roughly, a quarto is a book with relatively small pages, and a folio is a book with relatively large pages. More precisely: a quarto is made of sheets of paper, each of which has been folded twice to make four leaves (eight pages), whereas in a folio each sheet has been folded once to make two leaves (four pages).

2 Andrew Murphy: 'Introduction' to *The Tragœdie of Othello, the Moore of Venice* (Hemel Hempstead: Prentice Hall, Harvester Wheatsheaf, 1995), p. 13.

3 See, however, Honigmann's warning: 'Editors used to assume that F was purged because of the Act of Abuses, . . . but we now know that some scribes omitted profanity for purely "literary" reasons . . . ' (E. A. J. Honigmann: *The Texts of 'Othello' and Shakespearian Revision*; London and New York: Routledge, 1996; p. 3.)

4 Examples are: *Shakespeare's Quartos*, ed. Michael J. B. Allen and Kenneth Muir (Berkeley, Los Angeles and London: University of California Press, 1981); *The First Folio of Shakespeare*, ed. Charlton Hinman (1969; 2nd edn.: New York, Norton, 1996); and *The First Folios of Shakespeare*, ed. Doug Moston (New York: Applause, 1995).

THE TRAGEDY OF OTHELLO,
THE MOOR OF VENICE

CHARACTERS IN THE PLAY

OTHELLO, *the Moor, a general serving the Venetian state.*

DESDEMONA, *Othello's wife.*

BRABANTIO, *a Venetian senator and Desdemona's father.*

IAGO, *Othello's 'ancient' (ensign).*

EMILIA, *Iago's wife.*

CASSIO, *Othello's lieutenant.*

BIANCA, *a courtesan, Cassio's mistress.*

RODERIGO, *a Venetian gentleman.*

DUKE *of Venice.*

SENATORS *of Venice.*

MONTANO, *Governor of Cyprus.*

GRATIANO, *a noble Venetian, Desdemona's uncle.*

LODOVICO, *a noble Venetian, Desdemona's cousin.*

SAILOR.

CLOWN.

MESSENGER.

HERALD.

OFFICERS, GENTLEMEN, MUSICIANS *and* ATTENDANTS.

OTHELLO

ACT I, SCENE I.

Venice at night. A street.

Enter RODERIGO *and* IAGO.[1]

RODERIGO Tush, never tell me; I take it much unkindly
That thou, Iago, who hast had my purse
As if the strings were thine, shouldst know of this.

IAGO 'Sblood,[2] but you'll not hear me.
If ever I did dream of such a matter,
Abhor me.

RODERIGO Thou told'st me thou didst hold him in thy hate.

IAGO Despise me if I do not. Three great ones of the city,
In personal suit to make me his lieutenant,
Off-capped to him; and, by the faith of man,   10
I know my price: I am worth no worse a place.
But he, as loving his own pride and purposes,
Evades them with a bombast circumstance
Horribly stuffed with epithets of war;
And, in conclusion,
Nonsuits my mediators: for, 'Certes,' says he,
'I have already chose my officer.'
And what was he?
Forsooth, a great arithmetician,
One Michael Cassio, a Florentine,   20
A fellow almost damned in a fair wife,[3]
That never set a squadron in the field,
Nor the division of a battle knows
More than a spinster — unless the bookish theoric,
Wherein the toga'd consuls can propose
As masterly as he;[4] mere prattle without practice
Is all his soldiership. But he, sir, had th'election;
And I (of whom his eyes had seen the proof
At Rhodes, at Cyprus, and on other grounds
Christian and heathen) must be be-lee'd and calmed   30
By debitor-and-creditor.[5] This counter-caster,
He, in good time, must his lieutenant be,

And I, God bless the mark, His Moorship's ancient.[6]

RODERIGO   By heaven, I rather would have been his hangman.

IAGO   Why, there's no remedy: 'tis the curse of service;
Preferment goes by letter and affection,
And not by old gradation, where each second
Stood heir to th'first. Now, sir, be judge yourself
Whether I in any just term am affined
To love the Moor.

RODERIGO   I would not follow him then.   40

IAGO   O, sir, content you.
I follow him to serve my turn upon him.
We cannot all be masters, nor all masters
Cannot be truly followed. You shall mark
Many a duteous and knee-crooking knave
That, doting on his own obsequious bondage,
Wears out his time, much like his master's ass,
For nought but provender, and, when he's old, cashiered.
Whip me such honest knaves! Others there are
Who, trimmed in forms and visages of duty,   50
Keep yet their hearts attending on themselves;
And, throwing but shows of service on their lords,
Do well thrive by 'em; and, when they've lined
                        their coats,
Do themselves homage. These fellows have some soul,
And such a one do I profess myself – for sir,
It is as sure as you are Roderigo,
Were I the Moor, I would not be Iago;[7]
In following him, I follow but myself.
Heaven is my judge, not I for love and duty,
But seeming so, for my peculiar end;   60
For when my outward action doth demónstrate
The native act and figure of my heart
In compliment extern,[8] 'tis not long after
But I will wear my heart upon my sleeve
For daws to peck at. I am not what I am.

RODERIGO   What a full fortune does the thick-lips owe,
If he can carry't thus!

IAGO   Call up her father,
Rouse him, make after him, poison his delight,[9]

	Proclaim him in the streets, incense her kinsmen,
	And, though he in a fertile climate dwell,
	Plague him with flies; though that his joy be joy,
	Yet throw such changes of vexation on't
	As it may lose some colour.[10]
RODERIGO	Here is her father's house; I'll call aloud.
IAGO	Do, with like timorous accent and dire yell
	As when, by night and negligence, the fire
	Is spied in populous cities.[11]
RODERIGO	What, ho, Brabantio! Signior Brabantio, ho!
IAGO	Awake! What, ho, Brabantio! Thieves, thieves, thieves!
	Look to your house, your daughter, and your bags!
	Thieves, thieves!

Enter BRABANTIO *at a window above.*

BRABANTIO	What is the reason of this terrible summons?
	What is the matter there?
RODERIGO	Signior, is all your family within?
IAGO	Are your doors locked?
BRABANTIO	Why, wherefore ask you this?
IAGO	Zounds, sir, you're robbed; for shame, put on your gown;
	Your heart is burst; you have lost half your soul:
	Even now, now, very now, an old black ram
	Is tupping your white ewe! Arise, arise;
	Awake the snorting citizens with the bell,
	Or else the devil will make a grandsire of you.
	Arise, I say!
BRABANTIO	What, have you lost your wits?
RODERIGO	Most reverend signior, do you know my voice?
BRABANTIO	Not I; what are you?
RODERIGO	My name is Roderigo.
BRABANTIO	The worser welcome:
	I have charged thee not to haunt about my doors;
	In honest plainness thou hast heard me say
	My daughter is not for thee; and now, in madness,
	Being full of supper and distempering draughts,
	Upon malicious knavery dost thou come
	To start my quiet.

RODERIGO Sir, sir, sir —

BRABANTIO   But thou must needs be sure,
My spirit and my place have in them power
To make this bitter to thee.

RODERIGO   Patience, good sir.

BRABANTIO What tell'st thou me of robbing? This is Venice:
My house is not a grange.

RODERIGO   Most grave Brabantio,
In simple and pure soul I come to you.

IAGO Zounds, sir, you are one of those that will not serve
God if the devil bid you. Because we come to do you
service and you think we are ruffians, you'll have your 110
daughter covered with a Barbary horse; you'll have
your nephews neigh to you; you'll have coursers for
cousins, and jennets for germans.

BRABANTIO What profane wretch art thou?

IAGO I am one, sir, that comes to tell you, your daughter and
the Moor are now making the beast with two backs.[12]

BRABANTIO Thou art a villain.

IAGO   You are a senator.

BRABANTIO This thou shalt answer. I know thee, Roderigo.

RODERIGO Sir, I will answer anything. But I beseech you,
If't be your pleasure and most wise consent   120
(As partly I find it is) that your fair daughter,
At this odd-even and dull watch o'th'night,
Transported with no worse nor better guard
But with a knave of common hire, a gondolier,
To the gross clasps of a lascivious Moor —
If this be known to you, and your allowance,
We then have done you bold and saucy wrongs.
But if you know not this, my manners tell me
We have your wrong rebuke. Do not believe
That, from the sense of all civility,   130
I thus would play and trifle with your reverence.
Your daughter (if you have not given her leave),
I say again, hath made a gross revolt,
Tying her duty, beauty, wit and fortunes
In an extravagant and wheeling stranger
Of here and everywhere.[13] Straight satisfy yourself:

If she be in her chamber or your house,
Let loose on me the justice of the state
For thus deluding you.
BRABANTIO   Strike on the tinder, ho!
Give me a taper; call up all my people!   140
This accident is not unlike my dream;
Belief of it oppresses me already.
Light, I say, light!   [*Exit above.*
IAGO   Farewell, for I must leave you:
It seems not meet, nor wholesome to my place,
To be produced (as, if I stay, I shall)
Against the Moor; for I do know the state
(However this may gall him with some check)
Cannot with safety cast him, for he's embarked
With such loud reason to the Cyprus wars,[14]
Which even now stand in act, that, for their souls,   150
Another of his fathom they have none
To lead their business:[15] in which regard,
Though I do hate him as I do hell-pains,
Yet, for necessity of present life,
I must show out a flag and sign of love,
Which is indeed but sign. That you shall surely find him,
Lead to the Sagittary the raised search,[16]
And there will I be with him. So farewell.   [*Exit.*

Enter, below, BRABANTIO, *and* SERVANTS *with torches.*

BRABANTIO It is too true an evil. Gone she is,
And what's to come of my despisèd time   160
Is nought but bitterness. Now, Roderigo,
Where didst thou see her? (O unhappy girl!)
With the Moor, say'st thou? (Who would be a father!)
How didst thou know 'twas she? (O, she deceives me
Past thought!) What said she to you? – Get more tapers:
Raise all my kindred. – Are they married, think you?
RODERIGO Truly I think they are.
BRABANTIO O heaven, how got she out? O treason of the blood!
Fathers, from hence trust not your daughters' minds
By what you see them act. Is there not charms,   170
By which the property of youth and maidhood
May be abused? Have you not read, Roderigo,

          Of some such thing?

RODERIGO   Yes, sir: I have indeed.

BRABANTIO Call up my brother. – O, that you had had her! –
          Some one way, some another. – Do you know
          Where we may apprehend her and the Moor?

RODERIGO I think I can discover him, if you please
          To get good guard and go along with me.

BRABANTIO Pray you, lead on. At every house I'll call;
          I may command at most. Get weapons – ho! –   180
          And raise some special officers of night.
          On, good Roderigo; I'll deserve your pains.

                                          [Exeunt.

SCENE 2.

Another street.

Enter OTHELLO, IAGO, *and* ATTENDANTS *with torches.*

IAGO   Though in the trade of war I have slain men,
          Yet do I hold it very stuff o'th'conscience
          To do no contrived murder: I lack iniquity
          Sometimes to do me service. Nine or ten times
          I had thought t'have yerked him here, under the ribs.[17]

OTHELLO 'Tis better as it is.

IAGO   Nay, but he prated,
          And spoke such scurvy and provoking terms
          Against your honour
          That, with the little godliness I have,
          I did full hard forbear him. But I pray, sir,   10
          Are you fast married? For be sure of this,
          That the magnifico is much beloved,
          And hath in his effect a voice potential
          As double as the duke's: he will divorce you,
          Or put upon you what restraint and grievance
          The law, with all his might to enforce it on,
          Will give him cable.

OTHELLO   Let him do his spite;
          My services, which I have done the Signiory,
          Shall out-tongue his complaints. 'Tis yet to know –

Which, when I know that boasting is an honour,   20
I shall promúlgate[18] – I fetch my life and being
From men of royal siege; and my demerits
May speak unbonneted to as proud a fortune
As this that I have reached. For know, Iago,
But that I love the gentle Desdemona,[19]
I would not my unhousèd free condition
Put into circumscription and confine
For the sea's worth. But look, what lights come yond?

IAGO   Those are the raisèd father and his friends.
You were best go in.

OTHELLO   Not I: I must be found.   30
My parts, my title and my perfect soul
Shall manifest me rightly. Is it they?

IAGO   By Janus, I think no.[20]

Enter CASSIO *and* OFFICERS *with torches.*

OTHELLO   The servants of the duke, and my lieutenant?
The goodness of the night upon you, friends!
What is the news?

CASSIO   The duke does greet you, general,
And he requires your haste-post-haste appearance
Even on the instant.

OTHELLO   What is the matter, think you?

CASSIO   Something from Cyprus, as I may divine:
It is a business of some heat. The galleys   40
Have sent a dozen sequent messengers
This very night, at one another's heels;
And many of the consuls, raised and met,
Are at the duke's already. You have been hotly
                          called for;
When, being not at your lodging to be found,
The senate hath sent about three several quests
To search you out.

OTHELLO   'Tis well I am found by you.
I will but spend a word here in the house,
And go with you.   [*Exit.*

CASSIO   Ancient, what makes he here?

IAGO   Faith, he tonight hath boarded a land carack: 50
If it prove lawful prize, he's made for ever.

CASSIO	I do not understand.
IAGO	He's married.
CASSIO	To who?

Enter OTHELLO.

IAGO	Marry, to – Come, captain, will you go?
OTHELLO	Have with you.
CASSIO	Here comes another troop to seek for you.
IAGO	It is Brabantio. General, be advised:
	He comes to bad intent.

Enter BRABANTIO, RODERIGO, *and* OFFICERS *with torches and weapons.*

OTHELLO	Holla, stand there!
RODERIGO	Signior, it is the Moor.
BRABANTIO	Down with him, thief!

[*Both sides draw swords.*

IAGO	You, Roderigo! Come sir, I am for you.
OTHELLO	Keep up your bright swords, for the dew will rust
	them.

Good signior, you shall more command with years   60
Than with your weapons.

BRABANTIO O thou foul thief, where hast thou stowed my daughter?
Damned as thou art, thou hast enchanted her:[21]
For I'll refer me to all things of sense,
If she in chains of magic were not bound,[22]
Whether a maid so tender, fair, and happy,
So opposite to marriage that she shunned
The wealthy curlèd darlings of our nation,
Would ever have (t'incur a general mock)
Run from her guardage to the sooty bosom   70
Of such a thing as thou – to fear, not to delight.
Judge me the world, if 'tis not gross in sense
That thou hast practised on her with foul charms,
Abused her delicate youth with drugs or minerals
That weaken motion. I'll have't disputed on;
'Tis probable, and palpable to thinking.
I therefore apprehend and do attach thee[23]
For an abuser of the world, a practiser
Of arts inhibited and out of warrant.
Lay hold upon him; if he do resist,   80

Subdue him at his peril.

OTHELLO   Hold your hands,
Both you of my inclining and the rest:
Were it my cue to fight, I should have known it
Without a prompter. Where will you that I go
To answer this your charge?

BRABANTIO   To prison, till fit time
Of law, and course of direct session,
Call thee to answer.

OTHELLO   What if I do obey?
How may the duke be therewith satisfied,
Whose messengers are here about my side,
Upon some present business of the state,   90
To bring me to him?

OFFICER   'Tis true, most worthy signior;
The duke's in council, and your noble self,
I am sure, is sent for.

BRABANTIO   How? The duke in council?
In this time of the night? Bring him away:
Mine's not an idle cause: the duke himself,
Or any of my brothers of the state,
Cannot but feel this wrong as 'twere their own;
For if such actions may have passage free,
Bond-slaves and pagans shall our statesmen be.

                           [*Exeunt.*

SCENE 3.

A council-chamber.

The DUKE *and* SENATORS, *attended by* OFFICERS *with lights,
enter and sit at a table.*

DUKE   There is no composition in these news
That gives them credit.

SENATOR 1   Indeed they are disproportioned:
My letters say a hundred and seven galleys.

DUKE   And mine, a hundred forty.

SENATOR 2   And mine, two hundred;
But though they jump not on a just account –
As in these cases, where the aim reports,

            'Tis oft with difference – yet do they all confirm
            A Turkish fleet, and bearing up to Cyprus.
DUKE   Nay, it is possible enough to judgement:
            I do not so secure me in the error,   10
            But the main article I do approve
            In fearful sense.[24]
SAILOR   [outside:]   What ho, what ho, what ho!
OFFICER   A messenger from the galleys.

                  Enter SAILOR.

DUKE   Now, what's the business?
SAILOR   The Turkish preparation makes for Rhodes;
            So was I bid report here to the state
            By Signior Angelo.
DUKE   [to Senators:] How say you by this change?
SENATOR I   This cannot be,
            By no assay of reason; 'tis a pageant
            To keep us in false gaze. When we consider
            Th'importancy of Cyprus to the Turk,   20
            And let ourselves again but understand
            That, as it more concerns the Turk than Rhodes,
            So may he with more facile question bear it,
            For that it stands not in such warlike brace,
            But altogether lacks th'abilities
            That Rhodes is dressed in – if we make thought of this,
            We must not think the Turk is so unskilful
            To leave that latest which concerns him first,
            Neglecting an attempt of ease and gain
            To wake and wage a danger profitless.[25]   30
DUKE   Nay, in all confidence, he's not for Rhodes.
OFFICER   Here is more news.

                Enter a MESSENGER.

MESSENGER The Ottomites, reverend and gracious,
            Steering with due course toward the isle of Rhodes,
            Have there injointed with an after fleet.
SENATOR I Ay, so I thought; how many, as you guess?[26]
MESSENGER Of thirty sail; and now they do re-stem
            Their backward course, bearing with frank appearance
            Their purposes toward Cyprus. Signior Montano,

| | Your trusty and most valiant servitor, | 40 |

Your trusty and most valiant servitor,   40
With his free duty recommends you thus,
And prays you to believe him.[27]

DUKE   'Tis certain then for Cyprus.
             Marcus Luccicos, is not he in town?

SENATOR I   He's now in Florence.

DUKE   Write from us to him; post-post-haste dispatch.

SENATOR I   Here comes Brabantio and the valiant Moor.

Enter BRABANTIO, OTHELLO, IAGO, RODERIGO, CASSIO *and* OFFICERS.

DUKE   Valiant Othello, we must straight employ you
             Against the general enemy Ottoman.
             [*To Brabantio:*]
             I did not see you; welcome, gentle signior;   50
             We lacked your counsel and your help tonight.

BRABANTIO   So did I yours. Good your grace, pardon me:
             Neither my place nor aught I heard of business
             Hath raised me from my bed, nor doth the general care
             Take hold on me; for my particular grief
             Is of so flood-gate and o'erbearing nature
             That it engluts and swallows other sorrows,
             And yet is still itself.

DUKE   Why, what's the matter?

BRABANTIO   My daughter! O my daughter!

ALL   Dead?

BRABANTIO   Ay, to me:
             She is abused, stol'n from me, and corrupted   60
             By spells and medicines bought of mountebanks;
             For nature so preposterously to err
             (Being not deficient, blind, or lame of sense),
             Sans witchcraft could not.

DUKE   Whoe'er he be, that in this foul proceeding
             Hath thus beguiled your daughter of herself,
             And you of her, the bloody book of law
             You shall yourself read in the bitter letter
             After your own sense; yea, though our proper son
             Stood in your action.[28]

BRABANTIO   Humbly I thank your grace.   70
             Here is the man: this Moor, whom now, it seems,
             Your special mandate for the state affairs

              Hath hither brought.

ALL   We are very sorry for't.

DUKE   [*to Othello:*]
              What in your own part can you say to this?

BRABANTIO Nothing, but this is so.

OTHELLO   Most potent, grave, and reverend signiors,
              My very noble and approved good masters:
              That I have ta'en away this old man's daughter,
              It is most true; true, I have married her:
              The very head and front of my offending   80
              Hath this extent, no more. Rude am I in my speech,
              And little blest with the soft phrase of peace:
              For since these arms of mine had seven years' pith
              Till now some nine moons wasted, they have used
              Their dearest action in the tented field;
              And little of this great world can I speak
              More than pertains to feats of broil and battle;
              And therefore little shall I grace my cause
              In speaking for myself. Yet (by your gracious patience)
              I will a round unvarnished tale deliver   90
              Of my whole course of love: what drugs, what charms,
              What conjuration and what mighty magic
              (For such proceedings I am charged withal)
              I won his daughter.[29]

BRABANTIO   A maiden never bold;
              Of spirit so still and quiet that her motion
               Blushed at herself; and she – in spite of nature,
              Of years, of country, credit, everything –
              To fall in love with what she feared to look on?
              It is a judgement maimed and most imperfect
              That will confess perfection so could err   100
              Against all rules of nature, and must be driven
              To find out practices of cunning hell
              Why this should be. I therefore vouch again,
              That with some mixtures powerful o'er the blood,
              Or with some dram conjúred to this effect,
              He wrought upon her.

DUKE   To vouch this is no proof,
              Without more wider and more overt test

                 Than these thin habits and poor likelihoods
                 Of modern seeming do prefer against him.

SENATOR I But, Othello, speak: 110
                 Did you by indirect and forcèd courses
                 Subdue and poison this young maid's affections?
                 Or came it by request and such fair question
                 As soul to soul affordeth?

OTHELLO   I do beseech you,
                 Send for the lady to the Sagittary,
                 And let her speak of me before her father;
                 If you do find me foul in her report,
                 The trust, the office I do hold of you,[30]
                 Not only take away, but let your sentence
                 Even fall upon my life.

DUKE   [to officers:]   Fetch Desdemona hither.   120
OTHELLO   Ancient, conduct them; you best know the place.
                        [Exeunt Iago and officers.
                 And till she come, as truly as to heaven
                 I do confess the vices of my blood,
                 So justly to your grave ears I'll present
                 How I did thrive in this fair lady's love,
                 And she in mine.

DUKE   Say it, Othello.
OTHELLO   Her father loved me, oft invited me;
                 Still questioned me the story of my life
                 From year to year: the battles, sieges, fortunes,   130
                 That I have passed.
                 I ran it through, even from my boyish days
                 To th' very moment that he bade me tell it:
                 Wherein I spake of most disastrous chances,
                 Of moving accidents by flood and field,
                 Of hair-breadth scapes i'th'imminent deadly breach;
                 Of being taken by the insolent foe,
                 And sold to slavery; of my redemption thence,
                 And portance in my travels' history:
                 Wherein of antres vast and deserts idle,   ·   140
                 Rough quarries, rocks, and hills whose heads touch
                                     heaven,
                 It was my hint to speak: such was my process;

And of the cannibals that each other eat,
The Anthropophagi, and men whose heads
Do grow beneath their shoulders.[31] This to hear
Would Desdemona seriously incline;
But still the house affairs would draw her thence,
Which ever as she could with haste dispatch,
She'd come again, and with a greedy ear
Devour up my discourse; which I observing,   150
Took once a pliant hour, and found good means
To draw from her a prayer of earnest heart
That I would all my pilgrimage dilate,
Whereof by parcels she had something heard
But not intentively. I did consent,
And often did beguile her of her tears
When I did speak of some distressful stroke
That my youth suffered. My story being done,
She gave me for my pains a world of sighs:[32]
She swore, in faith 'twas strange, 'twas passing strange;   160
'Twas pitiful, 'twas wondrous pitiful;
She wished she had not heard it, yet she wished
That heaven had made her such a man.[33] She
                                                    thanked me,
And bade me, if I had a friend that loved her,
I should but teach him how to tell my story,
And that would woo her. Upon this hint I spake:
She loved me for the dangers I had passed,
And I loved her that she did pity them.
This only is the witchcraft I have used.
Here comes the lady; let her witness it.   170

    Enter DESDEMONA, IAGO *and* ATTENDANTS.

DUKE   I think this tale would win my daughter too.
              Good Brabantio,
              Take up this mangled matter at the best:
              Men do their broken weapons rather use
              Than their bare hands.

BRABANTIO   I pray you, hear her speak.
              If she confess that she was half the wooer,
              Destruction on my head, if my bad blame
              Light on the man. Come hither, gentle mistress:

Do you perceive in all this company
Where most you owe obedience?

DESDEM.   My noble father,   180
I do perceive here a divided duty.
To you I am bound for life and education;
My life and education both do learn me
How to respect you. You are the lord of duty;
I am hitherto your daughter. But here's my husband;
And so much duty as my mother showed
To you, preferring you before her father,
So much I challenge that I may profess
Due to the Moor my lord.

BRABANTIO   God buy: I've done.
Please it your grace, on to the state affairs.   190
I had rather to adopt a child than get it.
Come hither, Moor:
I here do give thee that with all my heart,
Which, but thou hast already, with all my heart [34]
I would keep from thee. — For your sake, jewel,
I am glad at soul I have no other child;
For thy escape would teach me tyranny,
To hang clogs on 'em. I have done, my lord.

DUKE   Let me speak like yourself,[35] and say a sentence
Which, as a grise or step, may help these lovers   200
Into your favour.
When remedies are past, the griefs are ended
By seeing the worst, which late on hopes depended.[36]
To mourn a mischief that is past and gone
Is the next way to draw new mischief on.
What cannot be preserved when Fortune takes,
Patience her injury a mockery makes.
The robbed that smiles steals something from the thief;
He robs himself that spends a bootless grief.

BRABANTIO So let the Turk of Cyprus us beguile;   210
We lose it not, so long as we can smile.
He bears the sentence well, that nothing bears
But the free comfort which from thence he hears;[37]
But he bears both the sentence and the sorrow,
That, to pay grief, must of poor patience borrow.

These sentences, to sugar or to gall,
Being strong on both sides, are equivocal.
But words are words: I never yet did hear
That the bruised heart was pierced through the ear.[38]
I humbly beseech you, proceed to th'affairs of state.   220

DUKE The Turk with a most mighty preparation makes for
Cyprus. Othello, the fortitude of the place is best
known to you; and though we have there a substitute
of most allowed sufficiency, yet opinion, a sovereign
mistress of effects, throws a more safer voice on you.
You must therefore be content to slubber the gloss of
your new fortunes with this more stubborn and bois-
terous expedition.

OTHELLO The tyrant Custom, most grave senators,
Hath made the flinty and steel couch of war   230
My thrice-driven bed of down. I do agnize
A natural and prompt alacrity
I find in hardness; and do undertake
These present wars against the Ottomites.
Most humbly therefore bending to your state,
I crave fit disposition for my wife,
Due reference of place and exhibition,
With such accommodation and besort
As levels with her breeding.

DUKE   If you please,
Be't at her father's.[39]

BRABANTIO   I'll not have it so.   240

OTHELLO Nor I.

DESDEM.   Nor I; I would not there reside,
To put my father in impatient thoughts
By being in his eye. Most gracious duke,
To my unfolding lend your prosperous ear,
And let me find a charter in your voice
T'assist my simpleness.

DUKE What would you, Desdemona?

DESDEM. That I did love the Moor to live with him,
My downright violence and scorn of fortunes[40]
May trumpet to the world. My heart's subdued   250
Even to the very quality of my lord.[41]

           I saw Othello's visage in his mind,
           And to his honours and his valiant parts
           Did I my soul and fortunes consecrate.
           So that, dear lords, if I be left behind,
           A moth of peace, and he go to the war,
           The rites for which I love him are bereft me,
           And I a heavy interim shall support
           By his dear absence. Let me go with him.

OTHELLO   Let her have your voice.   260
           Vouch with me, heaven, I therefore beg it not
           To please the palate of my appetite;
           Nor to comply with heat (the young affects
           In me defunct) and proper satisfaction;[42]
           But to be free and bounteous to her mind.
           And heaven defend your good souls that you think
           I will your serious and great business scant
           For she is with me. No, when light-winged toys
           Of feathered Cupid seel with wanton dullness
           My speculative and officed instruments,   270
           That my disports corrupt and taint my business,
           Let housewives make a skillet of my helm,
           And all indign and base adversities
           Make head against my estimation!

DUKE   Be it as you shall privately determine,
           Either for her stay or going; th'affair cries haste,
           And speed must answer it: you must hence tonight.

DESDEM.   Tonight, my lord?

DUKE   This night.

OTHELLO   With all my heart.[43]

DUKE   At nine i'th'morning, here we'll meet again.
           Othello, leave some officer behind,   280
           And he shall our commission bring to you
           With such things else of quality and respect
           As doth import you.

OTHELLO   So please your grace, my ancient:
           A man he is of honesty and trust;
           To his conveyance I assign my wife,
           With what else needful your good grace shall think
           To be sent after me.

DUKE   Let it be so.
Good night to everyone. And, noble signior,
If virtue no delighted beauty lack,
Your son-in-law is far more fair than black.   290

SENATOR I Adieu, brave Moor; use Desdemona well.

BRABANTIO Look to her, Moor, if thou hast eyes to see:
She has deceived her father, and may thee.[44]

        [Exeunt Duke, Brabantio, Cassio, Senators and officers.

OTHELLO My life upon her faith! Honest Iago,
My Desdemona must I leave to thee:
I prithee, let thy wife attend on her,
And bring them after in the best advantage.
Come, Desdemona, I have but an hour
Of love, of worldly matter and direction
To spend with thee: we must obey the time.   300

               [Exeunt Othello and Desdemona.

RODERIGO Iago!

IAGO What say'st thou, noble heart?

RODERIGO What will I do, think'st thou?

IAGO Why, go to bed and sleep.

RODERIGO I will incontinently drown myself.

IAGO If thou dost, I shall never love thee after. Why, thou
silly gentleman?

RODERIGO It is silliness to live, when to live is torment; and then
have we a prescription to die, when death is our
physician.   310

IAGO O villainous! I have looked upon the world for four
times seven years; and, since I could distinguish betwixt
a benefit and an injury, I never found a man that knew
how to love himself. Ere I would say I would drown
myself for the love of a guinea-hen, I would change
my humanity with a baboon.

RODERIGO What should I do? I confess it is my shame to be so
fond, but it is not in my virtue to amend it.

IAGO 'Virtue'? A fig! 'Tis in ourselves that we are thus or
thus. Our bodies are gardens, to the which our wills are   320
gardeners; so that if we will plant nettles or sow lettuce,
set hyssop and weed up tine,[45] supply it with one gender
of herbs or distract it with many, either to have it sterile

with idleness or manured with industry – why, the
power and corrigible authority of this lies in our wills. If
the balance of our lives had not one scale of reason to
poise another of sensuality, the blood and baseness of
our natures would conduct us to most preposterous
conclusions. But we have reason to cool our raging
motions, our carnal stings, our unbitted lusts: whereof   330
I take this, that you call love, to be a sect or scion.

RODERIGO It cannot be.

IAGO It is merely a lust of the blood and a permission of the
will. Come, be a man. Drown thyself? Drown cats and
blind puppies. I have professed me thy friend, and I
confess me knit to thy deserving with cables of perdurable
toughness. I could never better stead thee than now. Put
money in thy purse; follow thou these wars; defeat thy
favour with an usurped beard.[46] I say, put money in thy
purse. It cannot be that Desdemona should long continue   340
her love to the Moor – put money in thy purse – nor he
his to her: it was a violent commencement, and thou shalt
see an answerable sequestration – put but money in thy
purse. These Moors are changeable in their wills – fill thy
purse with money. The food that to him now is as
luscious as locusts, shall be to him shortly as bitter as
coloquintida. She must change for youth: when she is
sated with his body, she will find the error of her choice:
she must have change, she must. Therefore put money
in thy purse. If thou wilt needs damn thyself, do it a   350
more delicate way than drowning. Make all the money
thou canst. If sanctimony and a frail vow betwixt an
erring barbarian and a supersubtle Venetian be not too
hard for my wits and all the tribe of hell, thou shalt enjoy
her: therefore make money. A pox of drowning thyself;
it is clean out of the way. Seek thou rather to be hanged
in compassing thy joy[47] than to be drowned and go
without her.

RODERIGO Wilt thou be fast to my hopes, if I depend on the
issue?   360

IAGO Thou art sure of me; go, make money. I have told thee
often, and I retell thee again and again, I hate the Moor.

My cause is hearted; thine hath no less reason. Let us be
conjunctive in our revenge against him. If thou canst
cuckold him, thou dost thyself a pleasure, me a sport.
There are many events in the womb of time, which will
be delivered. Traverse, go; provide thy money. We will
have more of this tomorrow. Adieu.

RODERIGO Where shall we meet i'th'morning?

IAGO   At my lodging.   370

RODERIGO I'll be with thee betimes.

IAGO   Go to; farewell. Do you hear, Roderigo?

RODERIGO What say you?

IAGO   No more of drowning, do you hear?

RODERIGO I am changed.

IAGO   Go to; farewell. Put money enough in your purse.

RODERIGO I'll sell all my land.[48]   [*Exit.*

IAGO   Thus do I ever make my fool my purse;
          For I mine own gained knowledge should profane
          If I would time expend with such a snipe   380
          But for my sport and profit. I hate the Moor;
          And it is thought abroad that 'twixt my sheets
          He's done my office. I know not if't be true;
          Yet I, for mere suspicion in that kind,
          Will do as if for surety. He holds me well;
          The better shall my purpose work on him.
          Cassio's a proper man: let me see now;
          To get his place, and to plume up my will
          In double knavery. How? How? Let's see:
          After some time, to abuse Othello's ears   390
          That he is too familiar with his wife;
          He hath a person and a smooth dispose
          To be suspected – framed to make women false.
          The Moor is of a free and open nature,
          That thinks men honest that but seem to be so,
          And will as tenderly be led by th'nose
          As asses are.
          I have't: it is engendered. Hell and night
          Must bring this monstrous birth to the world's light.
                                                             [*Exit.*

ACT 2, SCENE I.

A sea-port in Cyprus.

Enter MONTANO *and two* GENTLEMEN, *one above.*

MONTANO What from the cape can you discern at sea?

GENT. 1 Nothing at all: it is a high-wrought flood;
        I cannot 'twixt the heaven and the main
        Descry a sail.

MONTANO Methinks the wind hath spoke aloud at land;
        A fuller blast ne'er shook our battlements.
        If it hath ruffianed so upon the sea,
        What ribs of oak, when mountains melt on them,
        Can hold the mortise? What shall we hear of this?

GENT. 2 A segregation of the Turkish fleet: 10
        For do but stand upon the foaming shore,
        The chidden billow seems to pelt the clouds;
        The wind-shaked surge, with high and monstrous mane,
        Seems to cast water on the burning Bear,
        And quench the guards of th'ever-fixèd Pole.
        I never did like molestation view
        On the enchafèd flood.

MONTANO   If that the Turkish fleet
        Be not ensheltered and embayed, they are drowned;
        It is impossible they bear it out.

Enter a third GENTLEMAN.

GENT. 3 News, lads! Our wars are done: 20
        The desperate tempest hath so banged the Turks
        That their designment halts. A noble ship of Venice
        Hath seen a grievous wreck and sufferance
        On most part of their fleet.

MONTANO How? Is this true?

GENT. 3   The ship is here put in,
        A Veronesa;[49] Michael Cassio,
        Lieutenant to the warlike Moor, Othello,
        Is come on shore; the Moor himself at sea,
        And is in full commission here for Cyprus.

| MONTANO | I am glad on't; 'tis a worthy governor. | 30 |

MONTANO I am glad on't; 'tis a worthy governor. 30

GENT. 3   But this same Cassio, though he speak of comfort
Touching the Turkish loss, yet he looks sadly,
And prays the Moor be safe; for they were parted
With foul and violent tempest.

MONTANO   Pray heaven he be;
For I have served him, and the man commands
Like a full soldier. Let's to the sea-side, ho! –
As well to see the vessel that's come in
As to throw out our eyes for brave Othello,
Even till we make the main and th'aerial blue
An indistinct regard.[50]

GENT. 3   Come, let's do so; 40
For every minute is expectancy
Of more arrivance.

Enter CASSIO.

CASSIO   Thanks to the valiant of this warlike isle,
That so approve the Moor! O, let the heavens
Give him defence against the elements,
For I have lost him on a dangerous sea.

MONTANO Is he well shipped?

CASSIO   His bark is stoutly timbered, and his pilot
Of very expert and approved allowance;
Therefore my hopes, not surfeited to death, 50
Stand in bold cure.

VOICE   [*offstage:*]   A sail, a sail, a sail!

CASSIO   What noise?

GENT. 2   The town is empty; on the brow o'th'sea
Stand ranks of people, and they cry 'A sail!'[51]

CASSIO   My hopes do shape him for the governor. [*Gun heard.*

GENT. 2   They do discharge their shot of courtesy:
Our friends at least.

CASSIO   I pray you, sir, go forth,
And give us truth who 'tis that is arrived.

GENT. 2   I shall.   [*Exit.*

MONTANO But, good lieutenant, is your general wived? 60

CASSIO   Most fortunately: he hath achieved a maid
That paragons description and wild fame;
One that excels the quirks of blazoning pens,

And in th'essential vesture of creation
Does tire the ingener.[52]

Enter second GENTLEMAN.

                    How now! Who has put in?

GENT. 2   'Tis one Iago, ancient to the general.

CASSIO   He's had most favourable and happy speed:
Tempests themselves, high seas, and howling winds,
The guttered rocks, and congregated sands,
Traitors insteeped to clog the guiltless keel,   70
As having sense of beauty, do omit
Their mortal natures, letting go safely by
The divine Desdemona.

MONTANO   What is she?

CASSIO   She that I spake of, our great captain's captain,
Left in the conduct of the bold Iago;
Whose footing here anticipates our thoughts
A se'nnight's speed. Great Jove, Othello guard,
And swell his sail with thine own powerful breath,
That he may bless this bay with his tall ship,
Make love's quick pants in Desdemona's arms,   80
Give renewed fire to our extincted spirits,
And bring all Cyprus comfort.

Enter DESDEMONA, EMILIA, IAGO *and* RODERIGO.

                      O behold,
The riches of the ship is come on shore!
You men of Cyprus, let her have your knees.
Hail to thee, lady; and the grace of heaven,
Before, behind thee, and on every hand,
Enwheel thee round!

DESDEM.   I thank you, valiant Cassio.
What tidings can you tell me of my lord?

CASSIO   He is not yet arrived; nor know I aught
But that he's well and will be shortly here.   90

DESDEM.   O, but I fear – How lost you company?

CASSIO   The great contention of the sea and skies
Parted our fellowship.

VOICE   [*offstage:*]   A sail, a sail!

CASSIO   But hark, a sail!   [*Gun heard.*

GENT. 2   They give their greeting to the citadel:
          This likewise is a friend.
CASSIO   See for the news.
                                        [*Exit Gentleman.*
          Good ancient, you are welcome.
          [*To Emilia:*]   Welcome, mistress.
          Let it not gall your patience, good Iago,
          That I extend my manners; 'tis my breeding
          That gives me this bold show of courtesy. [*He kisses her.* 100
IAGO   Sir, would she give you so much of her lips
          As of her tongue she oft bestows on me,
          You'd have enough.
DESDEM.   Alas, she has no speech.
IAGO   In faith, too much;
          I find it still when I have list to sleep.
          Marry, before your ladyship, I grant,
          She puts her tongue a little in her heart
          And chides with thinking.[53]
EMILIA   You have little cause to say so.
iago   Come on, come on; you are pictures out of doors,
          Bells in your parlours, wild-cats in your kitchens;   110
          Saints in your injuries, devils being offended;
          Players in your housewifery, and housewives in
          Your beds.[54]
DESDEM.   O, fie upon thee, slanderer!
IAGO   Nay, it is true, or else I am a Turk:
          You rise to play, and go to bed to work.
EMILIA   You shall not write my praise.
IAGO   No, let me not.
DESDEM.   What wouldst thou write of me, if thou shouldst
                                        praise me?
IAGO   O gentle lady, do not put me to't;
          For I am nothing if not critical.
DESDEM.   Come on, assay. – There's one gone to the harbour?   120
IAGO   Ay, madam.
DESDEM.   I am not merry; but I do beguile
          The thing I am by seeming otherwise.
          Come, how wouldst thou praise me?
IAGO   I am about it; but indeed my invention

Comes from my pate as birdlime does from frieze:[55]
It plucks out brains and all. But my muse labours,
And thus she is delivered:[56]
    If she be fair and wise, fairness and wit,
    The one's for use, the other useth it.   130

DESDEM. Well praised! How if she be black and witty?

IAGO   If she be black, and thereto have a wit,
    She'll find a white that shall her blackness hit.[57]

DESDEM. Worse and worse.

EMILIA   How if fair and foolish?

IAGO   She never yet was foolish that was fair,
    For even her folly helped her to an heir.

DESDEM. These are old fond paradoxes to make fools laugh
i'th'alehouse. What miserable praise hast thou for her
that's foul and foolish?   140

IAGO   There's none so foul, and foolish thereunto,
    But does foul pranks which fair and wise ones do.

DESDEM. O heavy ignorance: thou praisest the worst best. But
what praise couldst thou bestow on a deserving
woman indeed — one that in the authority of her merit
did justly put on the vouch of very malice itself?

IAGO   She that was ever fair, and never proud,
    Had tongue at will, and yet was never loud,
    Never lacked gold, and yet went never gay,
    Fled from her wish, and yet said 'Now I may';   150
    She that, being angered, her revenge being nigh,
    Bade her wrong stay, and her displeasure fly;
    She that in wisdom never was so frail
    To change the cod's head for the salmon's tail;[58]
    She that could think, and ne'er disclose her mind,
    See suitors following, and not look behind;[59]
    She was a wight, if ever such wight were —

DESDEM. To do what?

IAGO   To suckle fools and chronicle small beer.

DESDEM. O most lame and impotent conclusion! Do not learn of   160
him, Emilia, though he be thy husband. How say you,
Cassio? Is he not a most profane and liberal counsellor?

CASSIO He speaks home, madam. You may relish him more in
the soldier than in the scholar.   [*They converse quietly.*

IAGO   [*aside:*] He takes her by the palm. Ay, well said, whis-
            per. With as little a web as this will I ensnare as great a
            fly as Cassio. Ay, smile upon her, do; I will gyve thee
            in thine own courtship. You say true: 'tis so, indeed. If
            such tricks as these strip you out of your lieutenantry, it
            had been better you had not kissed your three fingers   170
            so oft, which now again you are most apt to play the sir
            in. Very good; well kissed, and excellent courtesy: 'tis
            so, indeed. Yet again, your fingers to your lips? Would
            they were clyster-pipes for your sake!

                                              [*Trumpets heard.*
            [*Aloud:*] The Moor! I know his trumpet.

CASSIO   'Tis truly so.

DESDEM.   Let's meet him and receive him.

CASSIO   Lo where he comes!

               Enter OTHELLO *and* ATTENDANTS.

OTHELLO   O my fair warrior!

DESDEM.   My dear Othello!

OTHELLO   It gives me wonder great as my content
            To see you here before me. O my soul's joy:
            If after every tempest come such calms,   180
            May the winds blow till they have wakened death,
            And let the labouring bark climb hills of seas
            Olympus-high, and duck again as low
            As hell's from heaven! If it were now to die,
            'Twere now to be most happy; for I fear,
            My soul hath her content so absolute
            That not another comfort like to this
            Succeeds in unknown fate.[60]

DESDEM.   The heavens forbid
            But that our loves and comforts should increase
            Even as our days do grow.

OTHELLO   Amen to that, sweet powers! 190
            I cannot speak enough of this content:
            It stops me here; it is too much of joy.
            [*They kiss.*] And this, and this, the greatest discords be
            That e'er our hearts shall make!

IAGO   [*aside:*] O, you are well tuned now; but I'll set down
            the pegs that make this music, as 'honest' as I am.[61]

OTHELLO   Come, let us to the castle.
           News, friends: our wars are done; the Turks are
                                                    drowned.
           How does my old acquaintance of this isle?
           (Honey, you shall be well desired in Cyprus;   200
           I have found great love amongst them. O my sweet,
           I prattle out of fashion, and I dote
           In mine own comforts.) I prithee, good Iago,
           Go to the bay, and disembark my coffers;
           Bring thou the master to the citadel –
           He is a good one, and his worthiness
           Does challenge much respect. Come, Desdemona,
           Once more, well met at Cyprus.
                              |*Exeunt all but Iago and Roderigo.*

IAGO   Do thou meet me presently at the harbour. Come
           hither. If thou be'st valiant (as they say base men,   210
           being in love, have then a nobility in their natures
           more than is native to them), list me. The lieutenant
           tonight watches on the court of guard. First, I must tell
           thee this: Desdemona is directly in love with him.

RODERIGO   With him? Why, 'tis not possible.

IAGO   Lay thy finger thus, and let thy soul be instructed. Mark
           me with what violence she first loved the Moor, but for
           bragging and telling her fantastical lies. And will she
           love him still for prating? Let not thy discreet heart
           think it. Her eye must be fed; and what delight shall she 220
           have to look on the devil? When the blood is made dull
           with the act of sport, there should be – again to inflame
           it and to give satiety a fresh appetite – loveliness in
           favour, sympathy in years, manners and beauties: all
           which the Moor is defective in. Now, for want of these
           required conveniences, her delicate tenderness will find
           itself abused, begin to heave the gorge, disrelish and
           abhor the Moor. Very Nature will instruct her in it and
           compel her to some second choice. Now sir, this
           granted (as it is a most pregnant and unforced position), 230
           who stands so eminent in the degree of this fortune as
           Cassio does – a knave very voluble; no further con-
           scionable than in putting on the mere form of civil and

humane seeming, for the better compassing of
his salt and most hidden loose affection? Why, none;
why, none! A slipper and subtle knave, a finder-out of
occasions; that has an eye can stamp and counterfeit
advantages, though true advantage never present itself.[62]
A devilish knave! Besides, the knave is handsome,
young, and hath all those requisites in him that folly and 240
green minds look after; a pestilent complete knave, and
the woman hath found him already.

RODERIGO I cannot believe that in her; she's full of most blest
condition.

IAGO Blest fig's-end! The wine she drinks is made of grapes.
If she had been blest, she would never have loved the
Moor. Blest pudding! Didst thou not see her paddle
with the palm of his hand? Didst not mark that?

RODERIGO Yes, that I did; but that was but courtesy.

IAGO Lechery, by this hand; an index and obscure prologue 250
to the history of lust and foul thoughts. They met so
near with their lips that their breaths embraced together. Villainous thoughts, Roderigo: when these
mutualities so marshal the way, hard at hand comes the
master and main exercise, th'incorporate conclusion.
Pish! But, sir, be you ruled by me. I have brought you
from Venice. Watch you tonight: for the command,
I'll lay't upon you. Cassio knows you not; I'll not be
far from you. Do you find some occasion to anger
Cassio, either by speaking too loud, or tainting his 260
discipline, or from what other course you please which
the time shall more favourably minister.

RODERIGO Well.

IAGO Sir, he's rash and very sudden in choler, and haply with
his truncheon may strike at you. Provoke him that he
may: for even out of that will I cause these of Cyprus to
mutiny, whose qualification shall come into no true
taste again but by the displanting of Cassio. So shall you
have a shorter journey to your desires, by the means I
shall then have to prefer them; and the impediment 270
most profitably removed, without the which there were
no expectation of our prosperity.

RODERIGO I will do this, if you can bring it to any opportunity.
IAGO   I warrant thee. Meet me by and by at the citadel. I
          must fetch his necessaries ashore. Farewell.
RODERIGO Adieu.   [*Exit.*
IAGO   That Cassio loves her, I do well believe't;
          That she loves him, 'tis apt and of great credit.
          The Moor (howbeit that I endure him not)
          Is of a constant, loving, noble nature;   280
          And I dare think he'll prove to Desdemona
          A most dear husband. Now I do love her too,
          Not out of absolute lust (though peradventure
          I stand accountant for as great a sin),
          But partly led to diet my revenge,
          For that I do suspect the lusty Moor
          Hath leaped into my seat: the thought whereof
          Doth like a poisonous mineral gnaw my inwards;
          And nothing can or shall content my soul
          Till I am evened with him, wife for wife;   290
          Or failing so, yet that I put the Moor
          At least into a jealousy so strong
          That judgement cannot cure. Which thing to do,
          If this poor trash of Venice, whom I trace
          For his quick hunting, stand the putting on,
          I'll have our Michael Cassio on the hip,[63]
          Abuse him to the Moor in the rank garb
          (For I fear Cassio with my night-cap too),
          Make the Moor thank me, love me, and reward me,
          For making him egregiously an ass,   300
          And practising upon his peace and quiet
          Even to madness. 'Tis here, but yet confused;
          Knavery's plain face is never seen till used.   [*Exit.*

SCENE 2.

A public place.

Enter Othello's HERALD *with a proclamation.*

HERALD   'It is Othello's pleasure' — our noble and valiant
general — 'that, upon certain tidings now arrived im-
porting the mere perdition of the Turkish fleet, every
man put himself into triumph: some to dance, some to
make bonfires, each man to what sport and revels his
addiction leads him: for, besides these beneficial news,
it is the celebration of his nuptial.' — So much was his
pleasure should be proclaimed. All offices are open, and
there is full liberty of feasting from this present hour of
five till the bell have told eleven. Heaven bless the isle 10
of Cyprus and our noble general Othello!

[*Exit.*

SCENE 3.

The citadel.

Enter OTHELLO, DESDEMONA, CASSIO *and* ATTENDANTS.

OTHELLO   Good Michael, look you to the guard tonight.
Let's teach ourselves that honourable stop,
Not to outsport discretion.

CASSIO   Iago hath direction what to do;
But notwithstanding, with my personal eye
Will I look to't.

OTHELLO   Iago is most honest.
Michael, good night. Tomorrow with your earliest
Let me have speech with you. [*To Desdemona:*]
                              Come, my dear love,
The purchase made, the fruits are to ensue;
That profit's yet to come 'tween me and you.   10
[*To Cassio:*] Good night.
                    [*Exeunt Othello, Desdemona and attendants.*

OTHELLO   65

Enter IAGO.

CASSIO   Welcome, Iago; we must to the watch.

IAGO   Not this hour, lieutenant: 'tis not yet ten o'clock. Our
         general cast us thus early for the love of his Desdemona;
         who let us not therefore blame: he hath not yet made
         wanton the night with her, and she is sport for Jove.

CASSIO   She's a most exquisite lady.

IAGO   And, I'll warrant her, full of game.

CASSIO   Indeed she's a most fresh and delicate creature.

IAGO   What an eye she has! Methinks it sounds a parley to   20
         provocation.

CASSIO   An inviting eye; and yet methinks right modest.

IAGO   And when she speaks, is it not an alarum to love?

CASSIO   She is indeed perfection.

IAGO   Well, happiness to their sheets! Come, lieutenant, I
         have a stoup of wine; and here without are a brace of
         Cyprus gallants that would fain have a measure to the
         health of black Othello.

CASSIO   Not tonight, good Iago; I have very poor and unhappy
         brains for drinking. I could well wish courtesy would   30
         invent some other custom of entertainment.

IAGO   O, they are our friends: but one cup; I'll drink for you.

CASSIO   I have drunk but one cup tonight, and that was craftily
         qualified too; and behold what innovation it makes
         here. I am unfortunate in the infirmity, and dare not
         task my weakness with any more.

IAGO   What, man! 'Tis a night of revels; the gallants desire it.

CASSIO   Where are they?

IAGO   Here, at the door; I pray you, call them in.

CASSIO   I'll do't; but it dislikes me.   [*Exit.* 40

IAGO   If I can fasten but one cup upon him,
         With that which he hath drunk tonight already,
         He'll be as full of quarrel and offence
         As my young mistress' dog. Now my sick fool Roderigo,
         Whom love hath turned almost the wrong side out,
         To Desdemona hath tonight caroused
         Potations pottle-deep; and he's to watch.
         Three else of Cyprus, noble swelling spirits
         That hold their honours in a wary distance,

The very elements of this warlike isle,[64]   50
Have I tonight flustered with flowing cups;
And they watch too. Now, 'mongst this flock of
                                    drunkards,
Am I to put our Cassio in some action
That may offend the isle. But here they come.

Enter CASSIO, MONTANO *and* GENTLEMEN.[65]

If consequence do but approve my dream,
My boat sails freely, both with wind and stream.

CASSIO   'Fore God, they have given me a rouse already.

MONTANO Good faith, a little one; not past a pint, as I am a soldier.

IAGO   Some wine, ho!

       [*He sings:*] 'And let me the canakin clink, clink;   60
               And let me the canakin clink.
                   A soldier's a man;
                   O, man's life's but a span;
                   Why then, let a soldier drink.'
       Some wine, boys!

CASSIO   'Fore God, an excellent song.

IAGO   I learned it in England, where indeed they are most
potent in potting. Your Dane, your German, and your
swag-bellied Hollander — drink, ho! — are nothing to
your English.   70

CASSIO   Is your Englishman so exquisite in his drinking?

IAGO   Why, he drinks you with facility your Dane dead drunk.
He sweats not to overthrow your Almain. He gives your
Hollander a vomit, ere the next pottle can be filled.

CASSIO   To the health of our general!

MONTANO I am for it, lieutenant; and I'll do you justice.

IAGO   O sweet England!

       [*He sings:*] 'King Stephen was and-a worthy peer,
               His breeches cost him but a crown;
                 He held them sixpence all too dear,   80
                   With that he called the tailor lown.

              He was a wight of high renown,
                 And thou art but of low degree;
             'Tis pride that pulls the country down;
                 Then take thy auld cloak about thee.'[66]
       Some wine, ho!

CASSIO   'Fore God, this is a more exquisite song than the other.

IAGO   Will you hear't again?

CASSIO   No; for I hold him to be unworthy of his place that
does those things. Well, God's above all; and there be   90
souls must be saved, and there be souls must not be
saved.

IAGO   It's true, good lieutenant.

CASSIO   For mine own part — no offence to the general, nor any
man of quality — I hope to be saved.

IAGO   And so do I too, lieutenant.

CASSIO   Ay, but, by your leave, not before me; the lieutenant is
to be saved before the ancient. Let's have no more of
this; let's to our affairs. God forgive us our sins! Gentlemen, let's look to our business. Do not think, 100
gentlemen, I am drunk: this is my ancient; this is my
right hand, and this is my left hand. I am not drunk
now: I can stand well enough, and I speak well enough.

ALL   Excellent well.

CASSIO   Why, very well then; you must not think then that I
am drunk.   [*Exit.*

MONTANO To th'platform, masters; come, let's set the watch.

                                     [*Exeunt gentlemen.*

IAGO   You see this fellow that is gone before:
He is a soldier fit to stand by Caesar
And give direction; and do but see his vice: 110
'Tis to his virtue a just equinox,
The one as long as th'other. 'Tis pity of him.
I fear, the trust Othello puts him in,
On some odd time of his infirmity
Will shake this island.

MONTANO   But is he often thus?

IAGO   'Tis evermore the prologue to his sleep:
He'll watch the horologe a double set,
If drink rock not his cradle.

MONTANO   It were well
The general were put in mind of it.
Perhaps he sees it not, or his good nature   120
Prizes the virtue that appears in Cassio,
And looks not on his evil: is not this true?

Enter RODERIGO.

IAGO   How now, Roderigo?
           I pray you, after the lieutenant; go.   [*Exit Roderigo.*
MONTANO   And 'tis great pity that the noble Moor
           Should hazard such a place as his own second
           With one of an ingraft infirmity.
           It were an honest action to say
           So to the Moor.
IAGO   Not I, for this fair island:
           I do love Cassio well, and would do much   130
           To cure him of this evil.
VOICE   [*offstage:*] Help! Help!
IAGO   But hark! What noise?

           Enter CASSIO, *pursuing* RODERIGO.

CASSIO   Zounds, you rogue, you rascal!
MONTANO   What's the matter, lieutenant?
CASSIO   A knave teach me my duty? I'll beat the knave into a
           twiggen bottle.
RODERIGO   Beat me?
CASSIO   [*He strikes Roderigo.*] Dost thou prate, rogue?
MONTANO   Nay, good lieutenant; pray sir, hold your hand.   140
CASSIO   Let go, sir, or I'll knock you o'er the mazard.
MONTANO   Come, come: you're drunk.
CASSIO   Drunk?   [*Cassio fights Montano.*
IAGO   [*aside to Roderigo:*]
           Away, I say; go out and cry a mutiny.   [*Exit Roderigo.*
           [*Aloud:*] Nay, good lieutenant! God's will, gentlemen!
           Help, ho! – Lieutenant – sir – Montano – sir –
           Help, masters! – Here's a goodly watch indeed!
                                                       [*A bell rings.*
           Who's that that rings the bell? – Diablo, ho!
           The town will rise. God's will, lieutenant, hold;
           You will be shamed for ever.   150

           Enter OTHELLO *and* ATTENDANTS.

OTHELLO   What is the matter here?
MONTANO   Zounds, I bleed still;
           I am hurt to th'death: he dies!   [*He assails Cassio.*
OTHELLO   Hold, for your lives!

IAGO　　　Hold, ho! Lieutenant – sir – Montano – gentlemen!
　　　　　Have you forgot all sense of place and duty?
　　　　　Hold, the general speaks to you; hold, for shame!

OTHELLO　Why, how now, ho? From whence ariseth this?
　　　　　Are we turned Turks, and to ourselves do that
　　　　　Which heaven hath forbid the Ottomites?[67]
　　　　　For Christian shame, put by this barbarous brawl.
　　　　　He that stirs next, to carve for his own rage,　　　160
　　　　　Holds his soul light: he dies upon his motion.
　　　　　Silence that dreadful bell; it frights the isle
　　　　　From her propriety. What's the matter, masters?
　　　　　Honest Iago, that look'st dead with grieving,
　　　　　Speak: who began this? On thy love, I charge thee.

IAGO　　　I do not know. Friends all but now, even now,
　　　　　In quarter and in terms like bride and groom
　　　　　Divesting them for bed; and then, but now
　　　　　(As if some planet had unwitted men),[68]
　　　　　Swords out, and tilting one at other's breast,　　　170
　　　　　In opposition bloody. I cannot speak
　　　　　Any beginning to this peevish odds;
　　　　　And would in action glorious I had lost
　　　　　Those legs that brought me to a part of it!

OTHELLO　How comes it, Michael, you are thus forgot?

CASSIO　　I pray you, pardon me; I cannot speak.

OTHELLO　Worthy Montano, you were wont be civil;
　　　　　The gravity and stillness of your youth
　　　　　The world hath noted, and your name is great
　　　　　In mouths of wisest censure: what's the matter,　　　180
　　　　　That you unlace your reputation thus,
　　　　　And spend your rich opinion, for the name
　　　　　Of a night-brawler? Give me answer to it.

MONTANO　Worthy Othello, I am hurt to danger;
　　　　　Your officer, Iago, can inform you –
　　　　　While I spare speech, which something now
　　　　　　　　　　　　　　　　　　　offends me –
　　　　　Of all that I do know; nor know I aught
　　　　　By me that's said or done amiss this night –
　　　　　Unless self-charity be sometimes a vice,
　　　　　And to defend ourselves it be a sin　　　190

When violence assails us.

OTHELLO   Now, by heaven,
My blood begins my safer guides to rule,
And passion, having my best judgment collied,
Assays to lead the way. Zounds, if I once stir,
Or do but lift this arm, the best of you
Shall sink in my rebuke. Give me to know
How this foul rout began, who set it on,
And he that is approved in this offence,
Though he had twinned with me, both at a birth,
Shall lose me. What! In a town of war,   200
Yet wild, the people's hearts brimful of fear,
To manage private and domestic quarrels,
In night, and on the court and guard of safety!
'Tis monstrous. Iago, who began't?[69]

MONTANO If partially affined, or leagued in office,[70]
Thou dost deliver more or less than truth,
Thou art no soldier.

IAGO   Touch me not so near;
I had rather have this tongue cut from my mouth
Than it should do offence to Michael Cassio;
Yet, I persuade myself, to speak the truth   210
Shall nothing wrong him. This it is, general:
Montano and myself being in speech,
There comes a fellow crying out for help,
And Cassio following with determined sword
To execute upon him. Sir, this gentleman
Steps in to Cassio and entreats his pause;
Myself the crying fellow did pursue,
Lest by his clamour (as it so fell out)
The town might fall in fright; he, swift of foot,
Outran my purpose; and I returned the rather   220
For that I heard the clink and fall of swords,
And Cassio high in oath; which till tonight
I ne'er might say before. When I came back –
For this was brief – I found them close together
At blow and thrust; even as again they were
When you yourself did part them.
More of this matter cannot I report;

But men are men: the best sometimes forget.
Though Cassio did some little wrong to him,
As men in rage strike those that wish them best,   230
Yet surely Cassio, I believe, received
From him that fled some strange indignity
Which patience could not pass.

OTHELLO   I know, Iago,
Thy honesty and love doth mince this matter,
Making it light to Cassio. Cassio, I love thee;
But never more be officer of mine.

            Enter DESDEMONA, *attended.*

Look if my gentle love be not raised up!
I'll make thee an example.

DESDEM.   What is the matter, dear?

OTHELLO   All's well now, sweeting;
Come away to bed. — Sir, for your hurts,   240
Myself will be your surgeon. Lead him off.

              [*Exeunt Montano and attendant.*

Iago, look with care about the town,
And silence those whom this vile brawl distracted.
Come, Desdemona: 'tis the soldiers' life
To have their balmy slumbers waked with strife.

              [*Exeunt all but Iago and Cassio.*

IAGO   What, are you hurt, lieutenant?

CASSIO   Ay, past all surgery.

IAGO   Marry, God forbid!

CASSIO   Reputation, reputation, reputation! O, I have lost my
reputation! I have lost the immortal part of myself,   250
and what remains is bestial. My reputation, Iago, my
reputation!

IAGO   As I am an honest man, I thought you had received
some bodily wound; there is more sense in that than in
reputation. Reputation is an idle and most false imposition; oft got without merit, and lost without deserving.
You have lost no reputation at all, unless you repute
yourself such a loser. What, man! There are ways to
recover the general again. You are but now cast in his
mood, a punishment more in policy than in malice;   260
even so as one would beat his offenceless dog to affright

an imperious lion. Sue to him again, and he's yours.

CASSIO   I will rather sue to be despised than to deceive so good a
commander with so light, so drunken, and so indiscreet
an officer. Drunk! And speak parrot! And squabble!
Swagger! Swear! And discourse fustian with one's own
shadow![71] O thou invisible spirit of wine, if thou hast no
name to be known by, let us call thee 'Devil'!

IAGO   What was he that you followed with your sword?
What had he done to you?   270

CASSIO   I know not.

IAGO   Is't possible?

CASSIO   I remember a mass of things, but nothing distinctly; a
quarrel, but nothing wherefore. O God, that men
should put an enemy in their mouths, to steal away
their brains; that we should, with joy, pleasance, revel
and applause, transform ourselves into beasts!

IAGO   Why, but you are now well enough: how came you
thus recovered?

CASSIO   It hath pleased the devil Drunkenness to give place to   280
the devil Wrath: one unperfectness shows me another,
to make me frankly despise myself.

IAGO   Come, you are too severe a moraller. As the time, the
place, and the condition of this country stands, I could
heartily wish this had not befallen; but since it is as it
is, mend it for your own good.

CASSIO   I will ask him for my place again; he shall tell me I am a
drunkard! Had I as many mouths as Hydra, such an
answer would stop them all. To be now a sensible man,
by and by a fool, and presently a beast! O strange! Every   290
inordinate cup is unblest, and the ingredience is a devil.

IAGO   Come, come: good wine is a good familiar creature, if
it be well used; exclaim no more against it. And, good
lieutenant, I think you think I love you.

CASSIO   I have well approved it, sir. – I drunk!

IAGO   You or any man living may be drunk at some time. I'll
tell you what you shall do. Our general's wife is now the
general: I may say so in this respect, for that he hath
devoted and given up himself to the contemplation,
mark and denotement of her parts and graces. Confess   300

yourself freely to her; importune her help to put you in
your place again. She is of so free, so kind, so apt, so
blessed a disposition, she holds it a vice in her goodness
not to do more than she is requested. This broken joint
between you and her husband entreat her to splinter;
and, my fortunes against any lay worth naming, this
crack of your love shall grow stronger than it was before.

CASSIO   You advise me well.

IAGO   I protest, in the sincerity of love and honest kindness.

CASSIO   I think it freely; and betimes in the morning, I will 310
            beseech the virtuous Desdemona to undertake for me.
            I am desperate of my fortunes if they check me here.

IAGO   You are in the right. Good night, lieutenant; I must to
            the watch.

CASSIO   Good night, honest Iago.   [Exit.

IAGO   And what's he then, that says I play the villain,
            When this advice is free I give, and honest,
            Probal to thinking, and indeed the course
            To win the Moor again? For 'tis most easy
            Th'inclining Desdemona to subdue   320
            In any honest suit. She's framed as fruitful
            As the free elements. And then for her
            To win the Moor: were't to renounce his baptism,
            All seals and symbols of redeemèd sin,
            His soul is so enfettered to her love
            That she may make, unmake, do what she list,
            Even as her appetite shall play the god
            With his weak function.⁷² How am I then a villain
            To counsel Cassio to this parallel course,
            Directly to his good? Divinity of hell!   330
            When devils will the blackest sins put on,
            They do suggest at first with heavenly shows,
            As I do now; for while this honest fool
            Plies Desdemona to repair his fortunes,
            And she for him pleads strongly to the Moor,
            I'll pour this pestilence into his ear,
            That she repeals him for her body's lust;
            And by how much she strives to do him good,
            She shall undo her credit with the Moor.

So will I turn her virtue into pitch,   340
And out of her own goodness make the net
That shall enmesh them all.

Enter RODERIGO.

                                        How now, Roderigo!

RODERIGO I do follow here in the chase, not like a hound that
hunts, but one that fills up the cry. My money is
almost spent; I have been tonight exceedingly well
cudgelled; and I think the issue will be, I shall have so
much experience for my pains; and so, with no money
at all and a little more wit, return again to Venice.

IAGO How poor are they that have not patience![73]
What wound did ever heal but by degrees?   350
Thou know'st we work by wit and not by witchcraft,
And wit depends on dilatory time.
Does't not go well? Cassio hath beaten thee,
And thou by that small hurt hast cashiered Cassio.
Though other things grow fair against the sun,
Yet fruits that blossom first will first be ripe.
Content thyself awhile. By th'Mass, 'tis morning;
Pleasure and action make the hours seem short.
Retire thee; go where thou art billeted;
Away, I say; thou shalt know more hereafter.   360
Nay, get thee gone.   [*Exit Roderigo.*
                        Two things are to be done:
My wife must move for Cassio to her mistress –
I'll set her on;
Myself a while to draw the Moor apart,
And bring him jump when he may Cassio find
Soliciting his wife. Ay, that's the way;
Dull not device by coldness and delay.

                                                [*Exit.*

ACT 3, SCENE 1.

The citadel. Outside Othello's lodging.

Enter CASSIO *and some* MUSICIANS.

CASSIO   Masters, play here; I will content your pains;
            Something that's brief; and bid 'Good morrow, general'.

                    They play. Enter CLOWN.

CLOWN   Why, masters, have your instruments been in Naples,
            that they speak i'th'nose thus?[74]   [*Playing ceases.*
MUSICIAN   How, sir, how?
CLOWN   Are these, I pray you, wind instruments?
MUSICIAN   Ay, marry, are they, sir.
CLOWN   O, thereby hangs a tail.
MUSICIAN   Whereby hangs a tale, sir?
CLOWN   Marry, sir, by many a wind instrument that I know.[75]   10
            But, masters, here's money for you; and the general so
            likes your music, that he desires you, for love's sake, to
            make no more noise with it.
MUSICIAN   Well, sir, we will not.
CLOWN   If you have any music that may not be heard, to't
            again; but (as they say) to hear music, the general does
            not greatly care.
MUSICIAN   We have none such, sir.
CLOWN   Then put up your pipes in your bag, for I'll away. Go;
            vanish into air; away!   [*Exeunt musicians.*   20
CASSIO   Dost thou hear, my honest friend?
CLOWN   No, I hear not your honest friend; I hear *you.*
CASSIO   Prithee, keep up thy quillets. There's a poor piece of gold
            for thee: if the gentlewoman that attends the general's
            wife be stirring, tell her there's one Cassio entreats her a
            little favour of speech. Wilt thou do this?
CLOWN   She is stirring, sir; if she will stir hither, I shall seem to
            notify unto her.
CASSIO   Do, good my friend.   [*Exit Clown.*

                    Enter IAGO.

                    In happy time, Iago.

IAGO	You have not been abed then?	30
CASSIO	Why, no; the day had broke before we parted.	
	I have made bold, Iago,	
	To send in to your wife: my suit to her	
	Is that she will to virtuous Desdemona	
	Procure me some access.	
IAGO	I'll send her to you presently;	
	And I'll devise a mean to draw the Moor	
	Out of the way, that your converse and business	
	May be more free.	
CASSIO	I humbly thank you for't. [*Exit Iago.*	
	I never knew	40
	A Florentine more kind and honest.	

Enter EMILIA.

EMILIA	Good morrow, good lieutenant. I am sorry	
	For your displeasure; but all will sure be well.	
	The general and his wife are talking of it,	
	And she speaks for you stoutly. The Moor replies	
	That he you hurt is of great fame in Cyprus	
	And great affinity, and that in wholesome wisdom	
	He might not but refuse you; but he protests he	
	loves you,	
	And needs no other suitor but his liking	
	To take the safest occasion by the front [76]	50
	To bring you in again.	
CASSIO	Yet, I beseech you,	
	If you think fit, or that it may be done,	
	Give me advantage of some brief discourse	
	With Desdemon alone.	
EMILIA	Pray you, come in:	
	I will bestow you where you shall have time	
	To speak your bosom freely.	
CASSIO	I am much bound to you.	
	[*Exeunt.*	

SCENE 2.

A room in the citadel.

Enter OTHELLO, IAGO *and* GENTLEMEN.

OTHELLO These letters give, Iago, to the pilot,
And by him do my duties to the senate.
That done, I will be walking on the works;
Repair there to me.

IAGO   Well, my good lord, I'll do't. [*Exit.*

OTHELLO This fortification, gentlemen, shall we see't?

GENT'MEN We'll wait upon your lordship.

[*Exeunt.*

SCENE 3.

Before the citadel.

Enter DESDEMONA, CASSIO *and* EMILIA.

DESDEM. Be thou assured, good Cassio, I will do
All my abilities in thy behalf.

EMILIA Good madam, do; I warrant it grieves my husband
As if the case were his.

DESDEM. O, that's an honest fellow. Do not doubt, Cassio,
But I will have my lord and you again
As friendly as you were.

CASSIO   Bounteous madam,
Whatever shall become of Michael Cassio,
He's never anything but your true servant.

DESDEM. I know't; I thank you. You do love my lord;   10
You have known him long; and be you well assured
He shall in strangeness stand no farther off
Than in a politic distance.[77]

CASSIO   Ay, but, lady,
That policy may either last so long,
Or feed upon such nice and waterish diet,
Or breed itself so out of circumstance,
That, I being absent, and my place supplied,

My general will forget my love and service.[78]

DESDEM.   Do not doubt that: before Emilia here
          I give thee warrant of thy place. Assure thee,   20
          If I do vow a friendship, I'll perform it
          To the last article. My lord shall never rest:
          I'll watch him tame,[79] and talk him out of patience;
          His bed shall seem a school, his board a shrift;
          I'll intermingle everything he does
          With Cassio's suit. Therefore be merry, Cassio;
          For thy solicitor shall rather die
          Than give thy cause away.

                    Enter OTHELLO *and* IAGO, *at a distance.*

EMILIA   Madam, here comes my lord.
CASSIO   Madam, I'll take my leave.   30
DESDEM.   Why, stay, and hear me speak.
CASSIO   Madam, not now: I am very ill at ease,
          Unfit for mine own purposes.
DESDEM.   Well, do your discretion.   [*Exit Cassio.*
IAGO   Ha! I like not that.
OTHELLO   What dost thou say?
IAGO   Nothing, my lord; or if — I know not what.
OTHELLO   Was not that Cassio parted from my wife?
IAGO   Cassio, my lord! No, sure, I cannot think it,
          That he would steal away so guilty-like,   40
          Seeing you coming.
OTHELLO   I do believe 'twas he.
DESDEM.   How now, my lord!
          I have been talking with a suitor here,
          A man that languishes in your displeasure.
OTHELLO   Who is't you mean?
DESDEM.   Why, your lieutenant, Cassio. Good my lord,
          If I have any grace or power to move you,
          His present reconciliation take;
          For if he be not one that truly loves you,
          That errs in ignorance and not in cunning,   50
          I have no judgment in an honest face.
          I prithee, call him back.
OTHELLO   Went he hence now?
DESDEM.   Ay, sooth; so humbled,

That he hath left part of his grief with me
To suffer with him. Good love, call him back.

OTHELLO Not now, sweet Desdemon; some other time.

DESDEM. But shall't be shortly?

OTHELLO   The sooner, sweet, for you.

DESDEM. Shall't be tonight at supper?

OTHELLO   No, not tonight.

DESDEM. Tomorrow dinner then?

OTHELLO   I shall not dine at home:
I meet the captains at the citadel.   60

DESDEM. Why then, tomorrow night; or Tuesday morn;
On Tuesday noon, or night; or Wednesday morn.
I prithee, name the time; but let it not
Exceed three days. In faith, he's penitent;
And yet his trespass, in our common reason
(Save that, they say, the wars must make example
Out of their best), is not almost a fault
T'incur a private check.[80] When shall he come?
Tell me, Othello. I wonder in my soul
What you would ask me that I should deny,   70
Or stand so mamm'ring on. What! Michael Cassio,
That came a-wooing with you, and, so many a time,
When I have spoke of you dispraisingly,
Hath ta'en your part – to have so much to do
To bring him in! Birlady, I could do much –

OTHELLO Prithee, no more. Let him come when he will;
I will deny thee nothing.

DESDEM.   Why, this is not a boon;
'Tis as I should entreat you wear your gloves,
Or feed on nourishing dishes, or keep you warm,
Or sue to you to do a peculiar profit   80
To your own person. Nay, when I have a suit
Wherein I mean to touch your love indeed,
It shall be full of poise and difficult weight,
And fearful to be granted.

OTHELLO   I will deny thee nothing.
Whereon, I do beseech thee, grant me this,
To leave me but a little to myself.

DESDEM. Shall I deny you? No; farewell, my lord.

OTHELLO	Farewell, my Desdemona; I'll come to thee straight.
DESDEM.	Emilia, come. – Be as your fancies teach you;
	Whate'er you be, I am obedient. 90

                    [Exeunt Desdemona and Emilia.

OTHELLO	Excellent wretch! Perdition catch my soul
	But I do love thee; and when I love thee not,
	Chaos is come again.[81]
IAGO	My noble lord –
OTHELLO	What dost thou say, Iago?
IAGO	Did Michael Cassio, when you wooed my lady,
	Know of your love?
OTHELLO	He did, from first to last:
	Why dost thou ask?
IAGO	But for a satisfaction of my thought;
	No further harm.
OTHELLO	Why of thy thought, Iago?
IAGO	I did not think he had been acquainted with her. 100
OTHELLO	O, yes, and went between us very oft.
IAGO	Indeed?
OTHELLO	'Indeed'? Ay, indeed. Discern'st thou aught in that?
	Is he not honest?
IAGO	'Honest', my lord?
OTHELLO	'Honest'? Ay, honest.
IAGO	My lord, for aught I know.
OTHELLO	What dost thou think?
IAGO	'Think', my lord?
OTHELLO	' "Think", my lord?' By heaven, thou echo'st me, 110
	As if there were some monster in thy thought
	Too hideous to be shown. Thou dost mean something:
	I heard thee say even now, thou lik'st not that,
	When Cassio left my wife. What didst not like?
	And when I told thee he was of my counsel
	In my whole course of wooing, thou criedst 'Indeed?',
	And didst contract and purse thy brow together,
	As if thou then hadst shut up in thy brain
	Some horrible conceit. If thou dost love me,
	Show me thy thought. 120
IAGO	My lord, you know I love you.
OTHELLO	I think thou dost;

And for I know thou'rt full of love and honesty,
And weigh'st thy words before thou giv'st them breath,
Therefore these stops of thine fright me the more:
For such things in a false disloyal knave
Are tricks of custom; but in a man that's just,
They're close dilations,[82] working from the heart
That passion cannot rule.

IAGO   For Michael Cassio,
I dare be sworn, I think that he is honest.

OTHELLO   I think so too.

IAGO   Men should be what they seem;   130
Or those that be not, would they might seem none.[83]

OTHELLO   Certain, men should be what they seem.

IAGO   Why then I think Cassio's an honest man.

OTHELLO   Nay, yet there's more in this.
I prithee, speak to me as to thy thinkings,
As thou dost ruminate, and give thy worst of thoughts
The worst of words.

IAGO   Good my lord, pardon me:
Though I am bound to every act of duty,
I am not bound to that all slaves are free to.[84]   140
Utter my thoughts? Why, say they are vile and false –
As where's that palace whereinto foul things
Sometimes intrude not? Who has a breast so pure,
But some uncleanly apprehensions
Keep lects and law-days, and in session sit
With meditations lawful?

OTHELLO   Thou dost conspire against thy friend, Iago,
If thou but think'st him wronged and mak'st his ear
A stranger to thy thoughts.

IAGO   I do beseech you,
Though I perchance am vicious in my guess
(As, I confess, it is my nature's plague   150
To spy into abuses, and oft my jealousy
Shapes faults that are not), that your wisdom then,
From one that so imperfectly conceits,
Would take no notice,[85] nor build yourself a trouble
Out of his scattering and unsure observance.
It were not for your quiet nor your good,

Nor for my manhood, honesty, or wisdom,
To let you know my thoughts.

OTHELLO   Zounds! What dost
                                      thou mean?

IAGO   Good name in man and woman, dear my lord,
Is the immediate jewel of their souls: 160
Who steals my purse, steals trash: 'tis something,
                                        nothing;
'Twas mine, 'tis his, and has been slave to thousands;
But he that filches from me my good name
Robs me of that which not enriches him
And makes me poor indeed.

OTHELLO   By heaven, I'll know
                                    thy thoughts!

IAGO   You cannot, if my heart were in your hand;
Nor shall not, while 'tis in my custody.

OTHELLO   Ha?

IAGO   O, beware, my lord, of jealousy:[86]
It is the green-eyed monster, which doth mock
The meat it feeds on. That cuckold lives in bliss   170
Who, certain of his fate, loves not his wronger;
But, O, what damnèd minutes tells he o'er,
Who dotes, yet doubts, suspects, yet fondly loves!

OTHELLO   O misery.

IAGO   Poor and content is rich, and rich enough;
But riches fineless is as poor as winter
To him that ever fears he shall be poor.
Good God the souls of all my tribe defend
From jealousy!

OTHELLO   Why, why is this?
Think'st thou I'd make a life of jealousy,   180
To follow still the changes of the moon
With fresh suspicions?[87] No; to be once in doubt
Is once to be resolved. Exchange me for a goat,[88]
When I shall turn the business of my soul
To such exsufflicate and blown surmises,
Matching thy inference. 'Tis not to make me jealous,
To say my wife is fair, feeds well, loves company,
Is free of speech, sings, plays and dances well;

            Where virtue is, these are more virtuous;

            Nor from mine own weak merits will I draw   190

            The smallest fear or doubt of her revolt;

            For she had eyes and chose me. No, Iago:

            I'll see before I doubt; when I doubt, prove;

            And on the proof, there is no more but this:

            Away at once with love or jealousy!

IAGO   I am glad of it; for now I shall have reason

            To show the love and duty that I bear you

            With franker spirit. Therefore, as I am bound,

            Receive it from me. I speak not yet of proof.

            Look to your wife; observe her well with Cassio;   200

            Wear your eye thus: not jealous nor secure:

            I would not have your free and noble nature

            Out of self-bounty be abused. Look to't.

            I know our country disposition well:

            In Venice they do let God see the pranks

            They dare not show their husbands; their best conscience

            Is not to leave't undone, but keep't unknown.

OTHELLO Dost thou say so?

IAGO   She did deceive her father, marrying you;

            And when she seemed to shake, and fear your looks,   210

            She loved them most.

OTHELLO   And so she did.

IAGO   Why, go to then:

            She that so young could give out such a seeming,

            To seel her father's eyes up close as oak,[89]

            He thought 'twas witchcraft – but I am much to blame;

            I humbly do beseech you of your pardon

            For too much loving you.

OTHELLO   I am bound to thee for ever.

IAGO   I see this hath a little dashed your spirits.

OTHELLO Not a jot, not a jot.

IAGO   I'faith, I fear it has.

            I hope you will consider what is spoke

            Comes from my love. But I do see you're moved.   220

            I am to pray you not to strain my speech

            To grosser issues nor to larger reach

            Than to suspicion.

OTHELLO	I will not.
IAGO	Should you do so, my lord,

My speech should fall into such vile success
As my thoughts aimed not at. Cassio's my worthy
                    friend – 90
My lord, I see you're moved.

OTHELLO   No, not much moved:
I do not think but Desdemona's honest.

IAGO   Long live she so, and long live you to think so!

OTHELLO   And yet, how nature erring from itself –   230

IAGO   Ay, there's the point: as (to be bold with you)
Not to affect many proposèd matches
Of her own clime, complexion, and degree,
Whereto we see in all things nature tends –
Foh! One may smell, in such, a will most rank,
Foul disproportion, thoughts unnatural.
But pardon me: I do not in position
Distinctly speak of her; though I may fear
Her will, recoiling to her better judgement,
May fall to match you with her country forms,   240
And happily repent.91

OTHELLO   Farewell, farewell.
If more thou dost perceive, let me know more;
Set on thy wife to observe. Leave me, Iago.

IAGO   [going:] My lord, I take my leave.

OTHELLO   (Why did I marry? This honest creature doubtless
Sees and knows more, much more, than he unfolds.)

IAGO   [returning:]
My lord, I would I might entreat your honour
To scan this thing no further. Leave it to time:
Although 'tis fit that Cassio have his place –
For sure he fills it up with great ability –   250
Yet if you please to hold him off awhile,
You shall by that perceive him and his means;
Note if your lady strain his entertainment
With any strong or vehement importunity:
Much will be seen in that. In the mean time,
Let me be thought too busy in my fears
(As worthy cause I have, to fear I am),

           And hold her free, I do beseech your honour.

OTHELLO Fear not my government.

IAGO   I once more take my leave.   [*Exit.* 260

OTHELLO This fellow's of exceeding honesty,

           And knows all qualities, with a learnèd spirit,

           Of human dealings. If I do prove her haggard,

           Though that her jesses were my dear heart-strings,

           I'd whistle her off and let her down the wind

           To prey at fortune.[92] Haply, for I am black,

           And have not those soft parts of conversation

           That chamberers have, or for I am declined

           Into the vale of years (yet that's not much),

           She's gone; I am abused, and my relief   270

           Must be to loathe her. O curse of marriage,

           That we can call these delicate creatures ours,

           And not their appetites! I had rather be a toad,

           And live upon the vapour of a dungeon,

           Than keep a corner in the thing I love

           For others' uses. Yet, 'tis the plague of great ones;

           Prerogatived are they less than the base;

           'Tis destiny unshunnable, like death:

           Even then this forkèd plague is fated to us

           When we do quicken.[93] Look where she comes;   280

               Enter DESDEMONA *and* EMILIA.

           If she be false, O then heaven mocks itself!

           I'll not believe 't.

DESDEM.   How now, my dear Othello?

           Your dinner, and the generous islanders

           By you invited, do attend your presence.

OTHELLO I am to blame.

DESDEM.   Why do you speak so faintly?

           Are you not well?

OTHELLO I have a pain upon my forehead, here.

DESDEM. Faith, that's with watching; 'twill away again.

           Let me but bind it hard, within this hour

           It will be well.

OTHELLO   Your napkin is too little;   290

         [*He pushes the handkerchief away, and it falls.*

          Let it alone. Come, I'll go in with you.

DESDEM.   I am very sorry that you are not well.

                      [Exeunt Othello and Desdemona.

EMILIA   I am glad I have found this napkin:
          This was her first remembrance from the Moor;
          My wayward husband hath a hundred times
          Wooed me to steal it; but she so loves the token
          (For he conjúred her she should ever keep it)
          That she reserves it evermore about her
          To kiss and talk to. I'll have the work ta'en out,
          And give't Iago. What he will do with it,   300
          Heaven knows, not I:
          I nothing, but to please his fantasy.

                 Enter IAGO.

IAGO   How now? What do you here alone?

EMILIA   Do not you chide; I have a thing for you.

IAGO   A 'thing' for me? It is a common thing –

EMILIA   Ha?

IAGO   To have a foolish wife.[94]

EMILIA   O, is that all? What will you give me now
          For that same handkerchief?

IAGO   What handkerchief?

EMILIA   'What handkerchief?'   310
          Why, that the Moor first gave to Desdemona;
          That which so often you did bid me steal.

IAGO   Hast stol'n it from her?

EMILIA   No, faith; she let it drop by negligence,
          And, to th'advantage, I being here took't up.
          Look, here it is.

IAGO   A good wench; give it me.

EMILIA   What will you do with't, that you've been so earnest
          To have me filch it?

IAGO   *[snatching it:]*   Why, what's that to you?

EMILIA   If't be not for some purpose of import,
          Give't me again. Poor lady, she'll run mad   320
          When she shall lack it.

IAGO   Be not acknown on't; I have use for it.
          Go, leave me.   *[Exit Emilia.*

I will in Cassio's lodging lose this napkin,
And let him find it. Trifles light as air
Are, to the jealous, confirmations strong
As proofs of holy writ. This may do something.
The Moor already changes with my poison:[95]
Dangerous conceits are in their natures poisons
Which at the first are scarce found to distaste,   330
But, with a little act upon the blood,
Burn like the mines of sulphur.[96]

Enter OTHELLO.

                         I did say so:
Look where he comes. Not poppy, nor mandragora,
Nor all the drowsy syrups of the world,
Shall ever medicine thee to that sweet sleep
Which thou owedst yesterday.

OTHELLO   Ha, ha, false to me?
IAGO   Why, how now, general? No more of that.
OTHELLO   Avaunt, be gone: thou hast set me on the rack!
I swear 'tis better to be much abused
Than but to know't a little.
IAGO   How now, my lord?   340
OTHELLO   What sense had I of her stol'n hours of lust?
I saw't not, thought it not; it harmed not me:
I slept the next night well, fed well, was free and merry;
I found not Cassio's kisses on her lips.
He that is robbed, not wanting what is stol'n,
Let him not know't, and he's not robbed at all.
IAGO   I am sorry to hear this.
OTHELLO   I had been happy, if the general camp,
Pioners and all, had tasted her sweet body,
So I had nothing known. O, now for ever,   350
Farewell the tranquil mind, farewell content;
Farewell the plumèd troops and the big wars
That make ambition virtue! O farewell;
Farewell the neighing steed and the shrill trump,
The spirit-stirring drum, th'ear-piercing fife,
The royal banner, and all quality,
Pride, pomp and circumstance of glorious war!
And O you mortal engines, whose rude throats

	Th'immortal Jove's dread clamours counterfeit,
	Farewell! Othello's occupation's gone! 360
IAGO	Is't possible, my lord?
OTHELLO	Villain, be sure thou prove my love a whore;
	Be sure of it; give me the ocular proof;
	Or by the worth of mine eternal soul,[97]
	Thou hadst been better have been born a dog
	Than answer my waked wrath!
IAGO	Is't come to this?
OTHELLO	Make me to see't; or, at the least, so prove it,
	That the probation bear no hinge nor loop
	To hang a doubt on; or woe upon thy life!
IAGO	My noble lord — 370
OTHELLO	If thou dost slander her and torture me,
	Never pray more; abandon all remorse;
	On horror's head horrors accumulate;
	Do deeds to make heaven weep, all earth amazed;
	For nothing canst thou to damnation add
	Greater than that.
IAGO	O grace! O heaven forgive me!
	Are you a man? Have you a soul, or sense?
	God buy you; take mine office. O wretched fool,
	That liv'st to make thine honesty a vice![98]
	O monstrous world! Take note, take note, O world, 380
	To be direct and honest is not safe.
	I thank you for this profit, and from hence
	I'll love no friend, sith love breeds such offence.
OTHELLO	Nay, stay; thou shouldst be honest.
IAGO	I should be wise; for honesty's a fool,
	And loses that it works for.
OTHELLO	By the world,
	I think my wife be honest, and think she is not;
	I think that thou art just, and think thou art not:
	I'll have some proof. Her name,[99] that was as fresh
	As Dian's visage, is now begrimed and black 390
	As mine own face. If there be cords, or knives,
	Poison, or fire, or suffocating streams,
	I'll not endure it. Would I were satisfied![100]
IAGO	I see, sir, you are eaten up with passion:

<table>
<tr><td></td><td>I do repent me that I put it to you.</td><td></td></tr>
<tr><td></td><td>You would be satisfied?</td><td></td></tr>
<tr><td>OTHELLO</td><td>Would? Nay I will.</td><td></td></tr>
<tr><td>IAGO</td><td>And may; but how? How satisfied, my lord?</td><td></td></tr>
<tr><td></td><td>Would you, the supervisor, grossly gape on –</td><td></td></tr>
<tr><td></td><td>Behold her topped?</td><td></td></tr>
<tr><td>OTHELLO</td><td>Death and damnation – O!</td><td></td></tr>
<tr><td>IAGO</td><td>It were a tedious difficulty, I think,</td><td>400</td></tr>
</table>

| | I do repent me that I put it to you. | |

OTHELLO   Would? Nay I will.

IAGO   And may; but how? How satisfied, my lord?
Would you, the supervisor, grossly gape on –
Behold her topped?

OTHELLO   Death and damnation – O!

IAGO   It were a tedious difficulty, I think,   400
To bring them to that prospect: damn them then,
If ever mortal eyes do see them bolster
More than their own. What then? How then?
What shall I say? Where's satisfaction?[101]
It is impossible you should see this,
Were they as prime as goats, as hot as monkeys,
As salt as wolves in pride, and fools as gross
As ignorance made drunk. But yet, I say,
If imputation and strong circumstances,
Which lead directly to the door of truth,   410
Will give you satisfaction, you may have't.

OTHELLO   Give me a living reason she's disloyal.

IAGO   I do not like the office;
But sith I am entered in this cause so far
(Pricked to't by foolish honesty and love),
I will go on. I lay with Cassio lately,
And, being troubled with a raging tooth,
I could not sleep.
There are a kind of men so loose of soul,
That in their sleeps will mutter their affairs: 420
One of this kind is Cassio.
In sleep I heard him say 'Sweet Desdemona,
Let us be wary, let us hide our loves';
And then, sir, would he gripe and wring my hand,
Cry out 'Sweet creature!', and then kiss me hard,
As if he plucked up kisses by the roots,
That grew upon my lips; then laid his leg
Over my thigh, and sighed, and kissed, and then
Cried 'Cursèd fate, that gave thee to the Moor!'

OTHELLO   O monstrous! Monstrous!

IAGO   Nay, this was but his dream. 430

OTHELLO	But this denoted a foregone conclusion:
	'Tis a shrewd doubt, though it be but a dream.[102]
IAGO	And this may help to thicken other proofs
	That do demónstrate thinly.
OTHELLO	I'll tear her all to pieces!
IAGO	Nay, but be wise: yet we see nothing done;
	She may be honest yet. Tell me but this:
	Have you not sometimes seen a handkerchief
	Spotted with strawberries in your wife's hand?
OTHELLO	I gave her such a one; 'twas my first gift.
IAGO	I know not that; but such a handkerchief
	(I am sure it was your wife's) did I today
	See Cassio wipe his beard with.
OTHELLO	If it be that —
IAGO	If it be that, or any that was hers,
	It speaks against her with the other proofs.
OTHELLO	O that the slave had forty thousand lives!
	One is too poor, too weak for my revenge.
	Now do I see 'tis true. Look here, Iago,
	All my fond love thus do I blow to heaven —
	'Tis gone.
	Arise, black vengeance, from thy hollow cell![103]
	Yield up, O love, thy crown and hearted throne
	To tyrannous hate! Swell, bosom, with thy fraught,
	For 'tis of aspics' tongues!
IAGO	Yet be content.
OTHELLO	O, blood, blood, blood!
IAGO	Patience, I say: your mind perhaps may change.
OTHELLO	Never, Iago. Like to the Pontic Sea,
	Whose icy current and compulsive course
	Ne'er feels retiring ebb, but keeps due on
	To the Propontic and the Hellespont;[104]
	Even so my bloody thoughts, with violent pace,
	Shall ne'er look back, ne'er ebb to humble love,
	Till that a capable and wide revenge
	Swallow them up. [*He kneels.*] Now, by yond
	marble heaven,[105]
	In the due reverence of a sacred vow

Line numbers: 440, 450, 460

         I here engage my words.

IAGO   Do not rise yet.   [*He kneels.*
         Witness, you ever-burning lights above,
         You elements that clip us round about,
         Witness that here Iago doth give up
         The execution of his wit, hands, heart,
         To wronged Othello's service! Let him command,   470
         And to obey shall be without remorse,
         What bloody business ever.[106]   [*They rise.*

OTHELLO   I greet thy love,
         Not with vain thanks, but with acceptance bounteous,
         And will upon the instant put thee to't:
         Within these three days let me hear thee say
         That Cassio's not alive.

IAGO   My friend is dead;
         'Tis done at your request. But let her live.

OTHELLO   Damn her, lewd minx: O, damn her, damn her!
         Come, go with me apart; I will withdraw
         To furnish me with some swift means of death   480
         For the fair devil. Now art thou my lieutenant.

IAGO   I am your own for ever.

                               [*Exeunt.*

SCENE 4.

The same location.

Enter DESDEMONA, EMILIA *and* CLOWN.

DESDEM.   Do you know, sirrah, where Lieutenant Cassio lies?

CLOWN   I dare not say he lies anywhere.

DESDEM.   Why, man?

CLOWN   He's a soldier; and for one to say a soldier lies, is
                stabbing.

DESDEM.   Go to; where lodges he?

CLOWN   To tell you where he lodges, is to tell you where I lie.

DESDEM.   Can anything be made of this?[107]

CLOWN   I know not where he lodges; and for me to devise a
                lodging, and say he lies here or he lies there, were to   10
                lie in mine own throat.

DESDEM. Can you inquire him out, and be edified by report?

CLOWN I will catechize the world for him: that is, make questions
       and by them answer.

DESDEM. Seek him; bid him come hither. Tell him I have moved
        my lord on his behalf, and hope all will be well.

CLOWN To do this is within the compass of man's wit, and
       therefore I will attempt the doing it.   [*Exit.*

DESDEM. Where should I lose that handkerchief, Emilia?

EMILIA I know not, madam.   20

DESDEM. Believe me, I had rather lose my purse
        Full of crusadoes; and but my noble Moor
        Is true of mind, and made of no such baseness
        As jealous creatures are, it were enough
        To put him to ill thinking.

EMILIA   Is he not jealous?

DESDEM. Who, he? I think the sun where he was born
        Drew all such humours from him.

                       Enter OTHELLO.

EMILIA   Look where he comes.

DESDEM. I will not leave him now till Cassio
        Be called to him. – How is't with you, my lord?

OTHELLO Well, my good lady. [*Aside:*] O, hardness to dissemble!   30
        – How do you, Desdemona?

DESDEM.   Well, my good lord.

OTHELLO Give me your hand. This hand is moist, my lady.

DESDEM. It yet hath felt no age, nor known no sorrow.

OTHELLO This argues fruitfulness and liberal heart:
        Hot, hot, and moist. This hand of yours requires
        A sequester from liberty: fasting and prayer,
        Much castigation, exercise devout;
        For here's a young and sweating devil, here,
        That commonly rebels. 'Tis a good hand,
        A frank one.

DESDEM.   You may, indeed, say so: 40
        For 'twas that hand that gave away my heart.

OTHELLO A liberal hand. The hearts of old gave hands;
        But our new heraldry is hands, not hearts.[108]

DESDEM. I cannot speak of this. Come now, your promise.

OTHELLO What promise, chuck?

DESDEM.   I have sent to bid Cassio come speak with you.

OTHELLO   I have a salt and sorry rheum offends me;
Lend me thy handkerchief.

DESDEM.   Here, my lord.

OTHELLO   That which I gave you.   50

DESDEM.   I have it not about me.

OTHELLO   Not?

DESDEM.   No, faith, my lord.

OTHELLO   That's a fault. That handkerchief
Did an Egyptian to my mother give;
She was a charmer, and could almost read
The thoughts of people. She told her, while she kept it
'Twould make her amiable and subdue my father
Entirely to her love; but if she lost it
Or made a gift of it, my father's eye   60
Should hold her loathly, and his spirits should hunt
After new fancies.[109] She, dying, gave it me,
And bid me, when my fate would have me wive,
To give it her. I did so; and take heed on't:
Make it a darling like your precious eye;
To lose't or give't away were such perdition
As nothing else could match.

DESDEM.   Is't possible?

OTHELLO   'Tis true. There's magic in the web of it:
A sibyl, that had numbered in the world
The sun to course two hundred compasses,[110]   70
In her prophetic fury sewed the work;
The worms were hallowed that did breed the silk;
And it was dyed in mummy, which the skilful
Conserved of maidens' hearts.[111]

DESDEM.   I'faith, is't true?[112]

OTHELLO   Most veritable; therefore look to't well.

DESDEM.   Then would to God that I had never seen't!

OTHELLO   Ha! Wherefore?

DESDEM.   Why do you speak so startingly and rash?

OTHELLO   Is't lost? Is't gone? Speak, is it out o'th'way?

DESDEM.   Heaven bless us!   80

OTHELLO   Say you?

DESDEM.   It is not lost; but what and if it were?

OTHELLO	How?
DESDEM.	I say it is not lost.
OTHELLO	Fetch't; let me see't.
DESDEM.	Why, so I can, sir, but I will not now.
	This is a trick to put me from my suit:
	Pray you, let Cassio be received again.
OTHELLO	Fetch me the handkerchief: my mind misgives.
DESDEM.	Come, come;
	You'll never meet a more sufficient man.
OTHELLO	The handkerchief.
DESDEM.	I pray, talk me of Cassio.
OTHELLO	The handkerchief.¹¹³
DESDEM.	A man that all his time
	Hath founded his good fortunes on your love,
	Shared dangers with you –
OTHELLO	The handkerchief!
DESDEM.	I'faith, you are to blame.
OTHELLO	Zounds!
EMILIA	Is not this man jealous?
DESDEM.	I ne'er saw this before.
	Sure, there's some wonder in this handkerchief:
	I am most unhappy in the loss of it.
EMILIA	'Tis not a year or two shows us a man:
	They are all but stomachs, and we all but food;
	They eat us hungerly, and when they are full
	They belch us.

90

[Exit.

100

Enter CASSIO *and* IAGO.

	Look you, Cassio and my husband.
IAGO	[*To Cassio:*] There is no other way: 'tis she must do't;
	And, lo, the happiness! Go and importune her.
DESDEM.	How now, good Cassio: what's the news with you?
CASSIO	Madam, my former suit. I do beseech you
	That, by your virtuous means, I may again
	Exist and be a member of his love
	Whom I with all the office of my heart
	Entirely honour. I would not be delayed:
	If my offence be of such mortal kind
	That nor my service past nor present sorrows,
	Nor purposed merit in futurity,

110

Can ransom me into his love again,
But to know so must be my benefit;
So shall I clothe me in a forced content
And shut myself up in some other course
To fortune's alms.[114]

DESDEM.   Alas, thrice-gentle Cassio,   120
My advocation is not now in tune;
My lord is not my lord; nor should I know him,
Were he in favour as in humour altered.[115]
So help me every spirit sanctified,
As I have spoken for you all my best
And stood within the blank of his displeasure
For my free speech. You must awhile be patient:
What I can do, I will; and more I will
Than for myself I dare. Let that suffice you.

IAGO   Is my lord angry?

EMILIA   He went hence but now,   130
And certainly in strange unquietness.

IAGO   Can he be angry? I have seen the cannon
When it hath blown his ranks into the air
And, like the devil, from his very arm
Puffed his own brother; and can he be angry?
Something of moment then: I will go meet him;
There's matter in't indeed, if he be angry.

DESDEM.   I prithee, do so.   [*Exit Iago.*
             Something sure of state,
Either from Venice, or some unhatched practice
Made demonstrable here in Cyprus to him,   140
Hath puddled his clear spirit; and in such cases
Men's natures wrangle with inferior things,
Though great ones are their object. 'Tis even so;
For let our finger ache, and it endues
Our other, healthful members even to that sense
Of pain. Nay, we must think men are not gods,
Nor of them look for such observancy
As fits the bridal.[116] Beshrew me much, Emilia:
I was (unhandsome warrior as I am)
Arraigning his unkindness with my soul;   150
But now I find I had suborned the witness,

And he's indicted falsely.[117]

EMILIA   Pray heaven it be state matters, as you think,
And no conception nor no jealous toy
Concerning you.

DESDEM.   Alas the day, I never gave him cause!

EMILIA   But jealous souls will not be answered so;
They are not ever jealous for the cause,
But jealous for they're jealous: 'tis a monster
Begot upon itself, born on itself.   160

DESDEM.   Heaven keep that monster from Othello's mind!

EMILIA   Lady, amen.

DESDEM.   I will go seek him. Cassio, walk hereabout:
If I do find him fit, I'll move your suit,
And seek to effect it to my uttermost.

CASSIO   I humbly thank your ladyship.

                        [*Exeunt Desdemona and Emilia.*

Enter BIANCA.

BIANCA   Save you, friend Cassio!

CASSIO   What make you from home?
How is it with you, my most fair Bianca?
I'faith, sweet love, I was coming to your house.

BIANCA   And I was going to your lodging, Cassio.   170
What, keep a week away? Seven days and nights,
Eight score eight hours, and lovers' absent hours,
More tedious than the dial eight score times:
O weary reckoning!

CASSIO   Pardon me, Bianca:
I have this while with leaden thoughts been pressed;
But I shall in a more continuate time
Strike off this score of absence. Sweet Bianca,

               [*He gives her Desdemona's handkerchief.*
Take me this work out.

BIANCA   O Cassio, whence came this?
This is some token from a newer friend:
To the felt absence now I feel a cause;   180
Is't come to this? Well, well.

CASSIO   Go to, woman!
Throw your vile guesses in the devil's teeth,
From whence you have them. You are jealous now

That this is from some mistress, some remembrance:
No, by my faith, Bianca.

BIANCA   Why, whose is it?

CASSIO   I know not, sweet: I found it in my chamber.
I like the work well. Ere it be demanded
(As like enough it will), I'd have it copied:
Take it, and do't; and leave me for this time.

BIANCA   Leave you? Wherefore?   190

CASSIO   I do attend here on the general;
And think it no addition, nor my wish,
To have him see me womaned.

BIANCA   Why, I pray you?

CASSIO   Not that I love you not.[118]

BIANCA   But that you do not love me.
I pray you, bring me on the way a little;
And say if I shall see you soon at night.

CASSIO   'Tis but a little way that I can bring you,
For I attend here; but I'll see you soon.

BIANCA   'Tis very good; I must be circumstanced.

                                        [*Exeunt.*

ACT 4, SCENE 1.

The same location.

Enter OTHELLO *and* IAGO.

IAGO   Will you think so?
OTHELLO   Think so, Iago?
IAGO   What,
           To kiss in private?
OTHELLO   An unauthorized kiss.
IAGO   Or to be naked with her friend in bed
           An hour, or more, not meaning any harm?
OTHELLO   Naked in bed, Iago, and not mean harm?
           It is hypocrisy against the devil:
           They that mean virtuously, and yet do so,
           The devil their virtue tempts, and they tempt heaven.
IAGO   If they do nothing, 'tis a venial slip;
           But if I give my wife a handkerchief –   10
OTHELLO   What then?
IAGO   Why, then, 'tis hers, my lord; and being hers,
           She may, I think, bestow't on any man.
OTHELLO   She is protectress of her honour too:
           May she give that?
IAGO   Her honour is an essence that's not seen;
           They have it very oft that have it not.[119]
           But for the handkerchief –
OTHELLO   By heaven, I would most gladly have forgot it.
           Thou said'st – O, it comes o'er my memory,   20
           As doth the raven o'er the infected house,
           Boding to all[120] – he had my handkerchief.
IAGO   Ay, what of that?
OTHELLO   That's not so good now.
IAGO   What
           If I had said I had seen him do you wrong?
           Or heard him say – as knaves be such abroad,
           Who having, by their own importunate suit
           Or voluntary dotage of some mistress,
           Convincèd or supplied them,[121] cannot choose

But they must blab —

OTHELLO   Hath he said anything?

IAGO   He hath, my lord; but, be you well assured,   30
      No more than he'll unswear.

OTHELLO   What hath he said?

IAGO   Faith, that he did — I know not what he did.

OTHELLO   What? What?

IAGO   Lie —

OTHELLO   With her?

IAGO   With her, on her; what you will.

OTHELLO   Lie with her! Lie on her! We say 'lie on her', when
      they belie her.[122] Lie with her: zounds, that's fulsome!
      Handkerchief — confessions — handkerchief! To confess,
      and be hanged for his labour. First, to be hanged, and
      then to confess.[123] I tremble at it. Nature would not
      invest herself in such shadowing passion without some   40
      instruction.[124] It is not words that shakes me thus. Pish!
      Noses, ears, and lips: is't possible? Confess? Handker-
      chief? O devil![125]   [*He falls in a trance.*

IAGO   Work on,
      My medicine, work! Thus credulous fools are caught;
      And many worthy and chaste dames even thus,
      All guiltless, meet reproach. — What, ho! My lord?
      My lord, I say! Othello!

Enter CASSIO.

How now, Cassio!

CASSIO   What's the matter?

IAGO   My lord is fall'n into an epilepsy.   50
      This is his second fit; he had one yesterday.

CASSIO   Rub him about the temples.

IAGO   No, forbear;
      The lethargy must have his quiet course;
      If not, he foams at mouth, and by and by
      Breaks out to savage madness. Look, he stirs.
      Do you withdraw yourself a little while.
      He will recover straight; when he is gone,
      I would on great occasion speak with you. [*Exit Cassio.*
      How is it, general? Have you not hurt your head?

OTHELLO	Dost thou mock me?
IAGO	I mock you? No, by heaven. 60

OTHELLO Dost thou mock me?

IAGO   I mock you? No, by heaven. 60
Would you would bear your fortune like a man!

OTHELLO A hornèd man's a monster and a beast.

IAGO There's many a beast then in a populous city,
And many a civil monster.

OTHELLO Did he confess it?

IAGO   Good sir, be a man:
Think every bearded fellow that's but yoked
May draw with you. There's millions now alive
That nightly lie in those unproper beds
Which they dare swear peculiar; your case is better.
O, 'tis the spite of hell, the fiend's arch-mock,   70
To lip a wanton in a secure couch,
And to suppose her chaste. No, let me know;
And knowing what I am, I know what she shall be.[126]

OTHELLO O, thou art wise; 'tis certain.

IAGO   Stand you awhile apart;
Confine yourself but in a patient list.
Whilst you were here o'erwhelmèd with your grief
(A passion most unsuiting such a man),
Cassio came hither. I shifted him away,
And laid good scuse upon your ecstasy;
Bade him anon return and here speak with me,   80
The which he promised. Do but encave yourself,
And mark the fleers, the gibes and notable scorns
That dwell in every region of his face:
For I will make him tell the tale anew,
Where, how, how oft, how long ago and when
He hath and is again to cope your wife.
I say, but mark his gesture. Marry, patience;
Or I shall say you're all-in-all in spleen,
And nothing of a man.

OTHELLO   Dost thou hear, Iago?
I will be found most cunning in my patience;   90
But – dost thou hear? – most bloody.

IAGO   That's not amiss;
But yet keep time in all. Will you withdraw?
                     [*Othello withdraws.*

Now will I question Cassio of Bianca,
A housewife that by selling her desires
Buys herself bread and clothes: it is a creature
That dotes on Cassio (as 'tis the strumpet's plague
To beguile many and be beguiled by one).
He, when he hears of her, cannot refrain
From the excess of laughter. Here he comes.

Enter CASSIO.

	As he shall smile, Othello shall go mad;	100
	And his unbookish jealousy must conster	
	Poor Cassio's smiles, gestures and light behaviour	
	Quite in the wrong. – How do you now, lieutenant?	
CASSIO	The worser, that you give me the addition	
	Whose want even kills me.	
IAGO	Ply Desdemona well, and you are sure on't.	
	[*Quietly:*] Now, if this suit lay in Bianca's power,	
	How quickly should you speed!	
CASSIO	Alas, poor caitiff!	
OTHELLO	Look how he laughs already.	
IAGO	I never knew a woman love man so.	110
CASSIO	Alas, poor rogue, I think, i'faith, she loves me.	
OTHELLO	Now he denies it faintly, and laughs it out.	
IAGO	Do you hear, Cassio?	
OTHELLO	Now he importunes him to tell it o'er.	
	Go to; well said, well said.	
IAGO	She gives it out that you shall marry her.	
	Do you intend it?	
CASSIO	Ha, ha, ha!	
OTHELLO	Do you triumph, Roman? Do you triumph?[127]	
CASSIO	I marry her? What, a customer?[128] I prithee, bear some 120 charity to my wit: do not think it so unwholesome. Ha, ha, ha!	
OTHELLO	So, so, so, so; they laugh that win.	
IAGO	Faith, the cry goes that you shall marry her.	
CASSIO	Prithee, say true.	
IAGO	I am a very villain else.	
OTHELLO	Have you scored me? Well.[129]	
CASSIO	This is the monkey's own giving out: she is persuaded	

I will marry her, out of her own love and flattery, not
out of my promise.   130

OTHELLO   Iago beckons me; now he begins the story.

CASSIO   She was here even now: she haunts me in every place.
I was the other day talking on the sea-bank with
certain Venetians; and thither comes the bauble, and,
by this hand, she falls thus about my neck —

OTHELLO   Crying 'O dear Cassio!' as it were: his gesture imports it.

CASSIO   So hangs, and lolls, and weeps upon me; so shakes, and
pulls me. Ha, ha, ha!

OTHELLO   Now he tells how she plucked him to my chamber. O, I
see that nose of yours, but not that dog I shall throw it to. 140

CASSIO   Well, I must leave her company.

IAGO   Before me! Look where she comes.

CASSIO   'Tis such another fitchew: marry, a perfumed one!

Enter BIANCA.

— What do you mean by this haunting of me?

BIANCA   Let the devil and his dam haunt you! What did you
mean by that same handkerchief you gave me even
now? I was a fine fool to take it. I must take out the
whole work? A likely piece of work, that you should
find it in your chamber and not know who left it
there! This is some minx's token, and I must take out 150
the work? There; give it your hobby-horse. Where-
soever you had it, I'll take out no work on't.

CASSIO   How now, my sweet Bianca, how now, how now?

OTHELLO   By heaven, that should be my handkerchief!

BIANCA   If you'll come to supper tonight, you may; if you will
not, come when you are next prepared for.   [*Exit.*

IAGO   After her, after her.

CASSIO   Faith, I must; she'll rail in the street else.

IAGO   Will you sup there?

CASSIO   Faith, I intend so.   160

IAGO   Well, I may chance to see you; for I would very fain
speak with you.

CASSIO   Prithee, come; will you?

IAGO   Go to; say no more.   [*Exit Cassio.*

OTHELLO   [*coming forward:*] How shall I murder him, Iago?

IAGO   Did you perceive how he laughed at his vice?

OTHELLO	O Iago!
IAGO	And did you see the handkerchief?
OTHELLO	Was that mine?
IAGO	Yours, by this hand — and to see how he prizes the 170 foolish woman your wife! She gave it him, and he hath given it his whore.[130]
OTHELLO	I would have him nine years a-killing. A fine woman, a fair woman, a sweet woman!
IAGO	Nay, you must forget that.
OTHELLO	Ay, let her rot, and perish, and be damned tonight; for she shall not live. No, my heart is turned to stone: I strike it, and it hurts my hand. O, the world hath not a sweeter creature: she might lie by an emperor's side and command him tasks.　　　　　　　　　180
IAGO	Nay, that's not your way.
OTHELLO	Hang her! I do but say what she is: so delicate with her needle, an admirable musician — O, she will sing the savageness out of a bear — of so high and plenteous wit and invention —
IAGO	She's the worse for all this.
OTHELLO	O, a thousand, thousand times — and then, of so gentle a condition!
IAGO	Ay, too gentle.
OTHELLO	Nay, that's certain; but yet the pity of it, Iago! O Iago, 190 the pity of it, Iago![131]
IAGO	If you are so fond over her iniquity, give her patent to offend; for, if it touch not you, it comes near nobody.
OTHELLO	I will chop her into messes — cuckold me!
IAGO	O, 'tis foul in her.
OTHELLO	With mine officer!
IAGO	That's fouler.
OTHELLO	Get me some poison, Iago, this night. I'll not expostulate with her, lest her body and beauty unprovide my mind again. This night, Iago.　　　　　　　　　200
IAGO	Do it not with poison: strangle her in her bed, even the bed she hath contaminated.
OTHELLO	Good, good: the justice of it pleases; very good.
IAGO	And for Cassio, let me be his undertaker: you shall hear more by midnight.

OTHELLO   Excellent good.   [*A trumpet sounds.*]
                    What trumpet is that same?
IAGO   Something from Venice, sure.

           Enter LODOVICO, DESDEMONA *and* ATTENDANTS.

                                        'Tis Lodovico,
           Come from the duke; and see, your wife is with him.
LODOVICO   God save the worthy general!
OTHELLO   With all my heart, sir.
LODOVICO   The duke and senators of Venice greet you.   210
                                        [*He gives Othello a letter.*
OTHELLO   I kiss the instrument of their pleasures.
                                        [*He opens it and reads.*
DESDEM.   And what's the news, good cousin Lodovico?
IAGO   I am very glad to see you, signior;
           Welcome to Cyprus.
LODOVICO   I thank you. How does Lieutenant Cassio?
IAGO   Lives, sir.
DESDEM.   Cousin, there's fall'n between him and my lord
           An unkind breach; but you shall make all well.
OTHELLO   Are you sure of that?
DESDEM.   My lord?   220
OTHELLO   [*reads:*] 'This fail you not to do, as you will . . . '
LODOVICO   He did not call; he's busy in the paper.
           Is there division 'twixt my lord and Cassio?
DESDEM.   A most unhappy one; I would do much
           T'atone them, for the love I bear to Cassio.
OTHELLO   Fire and brimstone!
DESDEM.   My lord?
OTHELLO   Are you wise?
DESDEM.   What, is he angry?
LODOVICO   May be the letter moved him;
           For, as I think, they do command him home,   230
           Deputing Cassio in his government.
DESDEM.   By my troth, I am glad on't.
OTHELLO   Indeed!
DESDEM.   My lord?
OTHELLO   'I am glad' − to see you mad.
DESDEM.   Why, sweet Othello!

OTHELLO	Devil! [*He strikes her.*
DESDEM.	I have not deserved this.
LODOVICO	My lord, this would not be believed in Venice,

Though I should swear I saw't. 'Tis very much.
Make her amends; she weeps.

OTHELLO   O devil, devil!
If that the earth could teem with women's tears,
Each drop she falls would prove a crocodile.   240
Out of my sight!

DESDEM.   I will not stay to offend you.

LODOVICO Truly, an obedient lady.
I do beseech your lordship, call her back.

OTHELLO Mistress!

DESDEM. My lord?

OTHELLO What would you with her, sir?

LODOVICO   Who, I, my lord?

OTHELLO Ay; you did wish that I would make her turn.
Sir, she can turn and turn, and yet go on
And turn again; and she can weep, sir, weep;
And she's obedient, as you say, obedient,   250
Very obedient. – Proceed you in your tears. –
Concerning this, sir, – O well-painted passion! –
I am commanded home. – Get you away;
I'll send for you anon. – Sir, I obey the mandate,
And will return to Venice. – Hence, avaunt! –
                       [*Exit Desdemona.*
Cassio shall have my place. And, sir, tonight,
I do entreat that we may sup together.
You are welcome, sir, to Cyprus. – Goats and monkeys!
                       [*Exit.*

LODOVICO Is this the noble Moor whom our full senate
Call all-in-all sufficient? Is this the nature   260
Whom passion could not shake, whose solid virtue
The shot of accident nor dart of chance
Could neither graze nor pierce?

IAGO   He is much changed.

LODOVICO Are his wits safe? Is he not light of brain?

IAGO   He's that he is. I may not breathe my censure.
What he might be – if what he might, he is not –

I would to heaven he were.[132]

LODOVICO   What, strike his wife!

IAGO   Faith, that was not so well; yet would I knew
        That stroke would prove the worst!

LODOVICO   Is it his use?
        Or did the letters work upon his blood,   270
        And new-create this fault?

IAGO   Alas, alas!
        It is not honesty in me to speak
        What I have seen and known. You shall observe him,
        And his own courses will denote him so
        That I may save my speech; do but go after,
        And mark how he continues.

LODOVICO I am sorry that I am deceived in him.

                                        [*Exeunt.*

SCENE 2.

A room in the citadel.

Enter OTHELLO *and* EMILIA.

OTHELLO You have seen nothing, then?

EMILIA   Nor ever heard, nor ever did suspect.

OTHELLO Yes, you have seen Cassio and she together.

EMILIA   But then I saw no harm, and then I heard
         Each syllable that breath made up between them.

OTHELLO What, did they never whisper?

EMILIA   Never, my lord.

OTHELLO Nor send you out o'th'way?

EMILIA   Never.

OTHELLO To fetch her fan, her gloves, her mask, nor nothing?

EMILIA   Never, my lord.   10

OTHELLO That's strange.

EMILIA   I durst, my lord, to wager she is honest,
         Lay down my soul at stake. If you think other,
         Remove your thought: it doth abuse your bosom.
         If any wretch have put this in your head,
         Let heaven requite it with the serpent's curse;[133]
         For if she be not honest, chaste, and true,

            There's no man happy: the purest of their wives
            Is foul as slander.

OTHELLO   Bid her come hither; go. [*Exit Emilia.*
            She says enough; yet she's a simple bawd   20
            That cannot say as much. This is a subtle whore,
            A closet lock and key of villainous secrets;[134]
            And yet she'll kneel and pray; I have seen her do't.

               Enter DESDEMONA *and* EMILIA.

DESDEM.   My lord, what is your will?
OTHELLO   Pray, chuck, come hither.
DESDEM.   What is your pleasure?
OTHELLO   Let me see your eyes:
            Look in my face.
DESDEM.   What horrible fancy's this?
OTHELLO   [*to Emilia:*] Some of your function, mistress.
            Leave procreants alone and shut the door;
            Cough, or cry 'hem', if anybody come:
            Your mystery, your mystery; nay, dispatch.   30
               [*Exit Emilia. Desdemona kneels.*
DESDEM.   Upon my knees, what doth your speech import?
            I understand a fury in your words,
            But not the words.
OTHELLO   Why, what art thou?
DESDEM.   Your wife, my lord; your true and loyal wife.
OTHELLO   Come, swear it, damn thyself;
            Lest, being like one of heaven, the devils themselves
            Should fear to seize thee. Therefore be double-damned:
            Swear thou art honest.
DESDEM.   Heaven doth truly know it.
OTHELLO   Heaven truly knows that thou art false as hell.   40
DESDEM.   To whom, my lord? With whom? How am I false?
OTHELLO   Ah, Desdemon, away, away, away!
DESDEM.   Alas the heavy day! Why do you weep?
            Am I the motive of these tears, my lord?
            If haply you my father do suspect
            An instrument of this your calling back,
            Lay not your blame on me; if you have lost him,
            Why, I have lost him too.
OTHELLO   Had it pleased heaven

To try me with affliction; had He rained
All kind of sores and shames on my bare head,   50
Steeped me in poverty to the very lips,
Given to captivity me and my utmost hopes,
I should have found in some place of my soul
A drop of patience; but, alas, to make me
A fixèd figure for the time of scorn
To point his slow-removing finger at![135]
Yet could I bear that too; well, very well;
But there, where I have garnered up my heart,
Where either I must live or bear no life,
The fountain from the which my current runs,   60
Or else dries up: to be discarded thence;
Or keep it as a cistern for foul toads
To knot and gender in![136] Turn thy complexion there,
Patience, thou young and rose-lipped cherubin,
Ay, there, look grim as hell![137]

DESDEM.   I hope my noble lord esteems me honest.
OTHELLO   O, ay; as summer flies are in the shambles,
That quicken even with blowing.[138] O thou weed,
Who art so lovely fair and smell'st so sweet
That the sense aches at thee . . . [139]   70
Would thou hadst ne'er been born!

DESDEM.   Alas, what ignorant sin have I committed?
OTHELLO   Was this fair paper, this most goodly book,
Made to write 'whore' upon? What 'committed'?
Committed! O thou public commoner,
I should make very forges of my cheeks,
That would to cinders burn up modesty,
Did I but speak thy deeds. What committed?[140]
Heaven stops the nose at it, and the moon winks;
The bawdy wind, that kisses all it meets,   80
Is hushed within the hollow mine of earth,[141]
And will not hear't. What committed! Impudent
                                        strumpet!

DESDEM.   By heaven, you do me wrong.
OTHELLO   Are not you a strumpet?
DESDEM.   No, as I am a Christian.
If to preserve this vessel for my lord

            From any other foul unlawful touch
            Be not to be a strumpet, I am none.

OTHELLO   What, not a whore?

DESDEM.   No, as I shall be saved.

OTHELLO   Is't possible?

DESDEM.   O, heaven forgive us!

OTHELLO   I cry you mercy then;   90
            I took you for that cunning whore of Venice
            That married with Othello.
            [*He calls Emilia:*]   You, mistress,
            That have the office opposite to Saint Peter,
            And keep the gate of hell!

                     Enter EMILIA.

                     You, you, ay, you.
            We've done our course; there's money for your pains:
            I pray you, turn the key, and keep our counsel.   [*Exit.*

EMILIA   Alas, what does this gentleman conceive?
            How do you, madam? How do you, my good lady?

DESDEM.   Faith, half asleep.

EMILIA   Good madam, what's the matter with my lord?   100

DESDEM.   With who?

EMILIA   Why, with my lord, madam.

DESDEM.   Who is thy lord?

EMILIA   He that is yours, sweet lady.[142]

DESDEM.   I have none. Do not talk to me, Emilia;
            I cannot weep, nor answers have I none
            But what should go by water. Prithee, tonight
            Lay on my bed my wedding sheets – remember;
            And call thy husband hither.

EMILIA   Here's a change indeed!
                                  [*Exit.*

DESDEM.   'Tis meet I should be used so, very meet.
            How have I been behaved, that he might stick   110
            The small'st opinion on my least misuse?[143]

                 Enter IAGO *and* EMILIA.

IAGO   What is your pleasure, madam? How is't with you?

DESDEM.   I cannot tell. Those that do teach young babes
            Do it with gentle means and easy tasks:

He might have chid me so; for, in good faith,
I am a child to chiding.

IAGO   What is the matter, lady?

EMILIA   Alas, Iago, my lord hath so bewhored her,
Thrown such despite and heavy terms upon her,
As true heart cannot bear.

DESDEM.   Am I that name, Iago?

IAGO   What name, fair lady?   120

DESDEM.   Such as she said my lord did say I was.

EMILIA   He called her whore: a beggar in his drink
Could not have laid such terms upon his callet.

IAGO   Why did he so?

DESDEM.   I do not know; I am sure I am none such.

IAGO   Do not weep, do not weep. Alas the day!

EMILIA   Hath she forsook so many noble matches,
Her father, and her country, and her friends,
To be called whore? Would it not make one weep?

DESDEM.   It is my wretched fortune.

IAGO   Beshrew him for't!   130
How comes this trick upon him?

DESDEM.   Nay, heaven
                                        doth know.

EMILIA   I will be hanged, if some eternal villain,
Some busy and insinuating rogue,
Some cogging, cozening slave, to get some office,
Have not devised this slander; I'll be hanged else.

IAGO   Fie, there is no such man: it is impossible.

DESDEM.   If any such there be, heaven pardon him!

EMILIA   A halter pardon him! And hell gnaw his bones!
Why should he call her whore? Who keeps her
                                        company?
What place, what time, what form, what likelihood?   140
The Moor's abused by some most villainous knave,
Some base notorious knave, some scurvy fellow.
O heaven, that such companions thou'dst unfold,
And put in every honest hand a whip
To lash the rascals naked through the world
Even from the east to th'west!

IAGO   Speak within door.

EMILIA   O, fie upon them! Some such squire he was
That turned your wit the seamy side without,
And made you to suspect me with the Moor.

IAGO   You are a fool; go to.

DESDEM.   Alas, Iago,   150
What shall I do to win my lord again?
Good friend, go to him; for, by this light of heaven,
I know not how I lost him. Here I kneel:
If e'er my will did trespass 'gainst his love
Either in discourse of thought or actual deed,
Or that mine eyes, mine ears, or any sense,
Delighted them in any other form,
Or that I do not yet, and ever did,
And ever will (though he do shake me off
To beggarly divorcement) love him dearly,   160
Comfort forswear me! Unkindness may do much;
And his unkindness may defeat my life,
But never taint my love. I cannot say 'whore':
It does abhor me now I speak the word;
To do the act that might the addition earn,
Not the world's mass of vanity could make me.[144]

IAGO   I pray you, be content; 'tis but his humour:
The business of the state does him offence,
And he does chide with you.

DESDEM.   If 'twere no other!

IAGO   'Tis but so, I warrant.   [*Trumpets sound.* 170
Hark how these instruments summon you to supper!
The messengers of Venice stay the meat.
Go in, and weep not; all things shall be well.

                    [*Exeunt Desdemona and Emilia.*

            Enter RODERIGO.

How now, Roderigo?

RODERIGO I do not find that thou deal'st justly with me.

IAGO   What in the contrary?

RODERIGO Every day thou doff'st me with some device, Iago; and
rather, as it seems to me now, keep'st from me all
conveniency, than suppliest me with the least advantage
of hope. I will indeed no longer endure it; nor am I 180

yet persuaded to put up in peace what already I have
foolishly suffered.

IAGO   Will you hear me, Roderigo?

RODERIGO Faith, I have heard too much; for your words and
performances are no kin together.

IAGO   You charge me most unjustly.

RODERIGO With naught but truth.[145] I have wasted myself out of
my means. The jewels you have had from me to
deliver to Desdemona would half have corrupted a
votarist. You have told me she hath received them, 190
and returned me expectations and comforts of sudden
respect and acquaintance; but I find none.

IAGO   Well; go to; very well.

RODERIGO 'Very well'; 'go to'! I cannot go to, man; nor 'tis not
very well. By this hand, I think 'tis very scurvy, and
begin to find myself fopped in it.

IAGO   Very well.

RODERIGO I tell you, 'tis *not* very well! I will make myself known
to Desdemona. If she will return me my jewels, I will
give over my suit and repent my unlawful solicitation; 200
if not, assure yourself I will seek satisfaction of you.

IAGO   You have said now.

RODERIGO Ay, and said nothing but what I protest intendment of
doing.

IAGO   Why, now I see there's mettle in thee; and even from
this instant do build on thee a better opinion than ever
before. Give me thy hand, Roderigo. Thou hast taken
against me a most just exception; but yet, I protest, I
have dealt most directly in thy affair.

RODERIGO It hath not appeared.   210

IAGO   I grant indeed it hath not appeared, and your suspicion
is not without wit and judgment. But, Roderigo, if thou
hast that in thee indeed, which I have greater reason to
believe now than ever (I mean purpose, courage, and
valour), this night show it. If thou the next night following enjoy not Desdemona, take me from this world
with treachery and devise engines for my life.

RODERIGO Well, what is it? Is it within reason and compass?

IAGO   Sir, there is especial commission come from Venice to
             depute Cassio in Othello's place.   220

RODERIGO Is that true? Why then, Othello and Desdemona return
             again to Venice.

IAGO   O no; he goes into Mauritania, and takes away with
             him the fair Desdemona, unless his abode be lingered
             here by some accident: wherein none can be so deter-
             minate as the removing of Cassio.

RODERIGO How do you mean, 'removing' of him?

IAGO   Why, by making him uncapable of Othello's place:
             knocking out his brains.

RODERIGO And that you would have me do?   230

IAGO   Ay, if you dare do yourself a profit and a right. He sups
             tonight with a harlotry, and thither will I go to him.
             He knows not yet of his honourable fortune. If you
             will watch his going thence, which I will fashion to fall
             out between twelve and one, you may take him at
             your pleasure. I will be near to second your attempt,
             and he shall fall between us. Come, stand not amazed
             at it, but go along with me; I will show you such a
             necessity in his death, that you shall think yourself
             bound to put it on him. It is now high supper-time, 240
             and the night grows to waste. About it.

RODERIGO I will hear further reason for this.

IAGO   And you shall be satisfied.

                                         [*Exeunt.*

SCENE 3.

Another room in the citadel.

Enter OTHELLO, LODOVICO, DESDEMONA, EMILIA *and* ATTENDANTS.

LODOVICO I do beseech you, sir, trouble yourself no further.

OTHELLO O pardon me; 'twill do me good to walk.

LODOVICO Madam, good night; I humbly thank your ladyship.

DESDEM. Your honour is most welcome.

OTHELLO   Will you walk, sir?
          O, Desdemona!

DESDEM. My lord?

OTHELLO	Get you to bed on th'instant; I will be returned forth- with. Dismiss your attendant there: look't be done.
DESDEM.	I will, my lord. [*Exeunt Othello, Lodovico and attendants.*
EMILIA	How goes it now? He looks gentler than he did. 10
DESDEM.	He says he will return incontinent: He hath commanded me to go to bed, And bade me to dismiss you.
EMILIA	Dismiss me?
DESDEM.	It was his bidding; therefore, good Emilia, Give me my nightly wearing, and adieu: We must not now displease him.
EMILIA	I would you had never seen him!
DESDEM.	So would not I: my love doth so approve him, That even his stubbornness, his checks, his frowns – Prithee, unpin me – have grace and favour in them. 20
EMILIA	I have laid those sheets you bade me on the bed.
DESDEM.	All's one. Good faith, how foolish are our minds! If I do die before thee, prithee shroud me In one of those same sheets.
EMILIA	Come, come, you talk.
DESDEM.	My mother had a maid called Barbary. She was in love; and he she loved proved mad, And did forsake her. She had a song of 'willow': An old thing 'twas, but it expressed her fortune, And she died singing it. That song tonight Will not go from my mind. I have much to do 30 But to go hang my head all at one side And sing it like poor Barbary. Prithee, dispatch.
EMILIA	Shall I go fetch your night-gown?
DESDEM.	No, unpin me here. This Lodovico is a proper man.
EMILIA	A very handsome man.
DESDEM.	He speaks well.
EMILIA	I know a lady in Venice would have walked barefoot to Palestine for a touch of his nether lip.

DESDEM.	[*sings:*] 'The poor soul sat sighing by a sycamore tree,
	        Sing all a green willow;
	            Her hand on her bosom, her head on her knee, 40
	                Sing willow, willow, willow;

The fresh streams ran by her, and murmured
her moans;
Sing willow, willow, willow;
Her salt tears fell from her, and softened the
stones,
Sing willow,'
– Lay by these –
'willow, willow;'
– Prithee, hie thee; he'll come anon –
   ' "Sing all, a green willow must be my garland. 50
   Let nobody blame him; his scorn I approve"'
– Nay, that's not next.[146] Hark! Who is't that knocks?

EMILIA   It's the wind.

DESDEM. |*sings:*| ' "I called my love false love; but what said
he then?
Sing willow, willow, willow;
   'If I court moe women, you'll couch with
moe men.' " '[147]

So, get thee gone; good night. Mine eyes do itch;
Does that bode weeping?

EMILIA   'Tis neither here nor there.

DESDEM.   I have heard it said so. O, these men, these men!
Dost thou in conscience think – tell me, Emilia   60
That there be women do abuse their husbands
In such gross kind?

EMILIA   There be some such, no question.[148]

DESDEM.   Wouldst thou do such a deed for all the world?

EMILIA   Why, would not you?

DESDEM.   No, by this heavenly light![149]

EMILIA   Nor I neither by this heavenly light: I might do't as well
i'th'dark.

DESDEM.   Wouldst thou do such a deed for all the world?

EMILIA   The world's a huge thing: it is a great prize for a small
vice.

DESDEM.   Good troth, I think thou wouldst not.   70

EMILIA   By my troth, I think I should; and undo't when I had
done it. Marry, I would not do such a thing for a joint-
ring, nor for measures of lawn, nor for gowns,
petticoats, nor caps, nor any petty exhibition. But for all

the whole world – Ud's pity, who would not make her
husband a cuckold, to make him a monarch? I should
venture purgatory for't.

DESDEM. Beshrew me, if I would do such a wrong for the whole
world.

EMILIA   Why, the wrong is but a wrong i'th'world; and having 80
the world for your labour, 'tis a wrong in your own
world, and you might quickly make it right.

DESDEM. I do not think there is any such woman.

EMILIA   Yes, a dozen; and as many to th'vantage as would store
the world they played for.
But I do think it is their husbands' faults
If wives do fall. Say that they slack their duties
And pour our treasures into foreign laps,[150]
Or else break out in peevish jealousies,
Throwing restraint upon us; or say they strike us,   90
Or scant our former having in despite –[151]
Why, we have galls, and though we have some grace,
Yet have we some revenge. Let husbands know
Their wives have sense like them: they see, and smell,
And have their palates both for sweet and sour,
As husbands have. What is it that they do,
When they change us for others? Is it sport?
I think it is. And doth affection breed it?
I think it doth. Is't frailty that thus errs?
It is so too. And have not we affections,   100
Desires for sport, and frailty, as men have?
Then let them use us well; else let them know,
The ills we do, their ills instruct us so.[152]

DESDEM. Good night, good night. God me such usage send:
Not to pick bad from bad, but by bad mend!

                                                    [*Exeunt.*

ACT 5, SCENE I.

Night. A street.

Enter IAGO *and* RODERIGO.

IAGO   Here, stand behind this bulk; straight will he come.
Wear thy good rapier bare, and put it home;
Quick, quick; fear nothing; I'll be at thy elbow.
It makes us, or it mars us; think on that,
And fix most firm thy resolution.

RODERIGO Be near at hand; I may miscarry in't.

IAGO   Here, at thy hand. Be bold, and take thy stand.
                          [*He withdraws.*

RODERIGO I have no great devotion to the deed,
And yet he hath given me satisfying reasons.
'Tis but a man gone. Forth, my sword: he dies.   10

IAGO   I have rubbed this young quat almost to the sense,
And he grows angry. Now, whether he kill Cassio,
Or Cassio him, or each do kill the other,
Every way makes my gain. Live Roderigo,
He calls me to a restitution large
Of gold and jewels that I bobbed from him
As gifts to Desdemona.
It must not be. If Cassio do remain,
He hath a daily beauty in his life
That makes me ugly; and besides, the Moor   20
May unfold me to him: there stand I in much peril.
No, he must die. Be't so. I hear him coming.

Enter CASSIO.

RODERIGO I know his gait: 'tis he. Villain, thou diest!
        [*He thrusts his rapier at Cassio, who then draws.*

CASSIO   That thrust had been mine enemy indeed,
But that my coat is better than thou think'st.
I will make proof of thine.   [*He wounds Roderigo.*

RODERIGO   O, I am slain!
    [*Iago from behind strikes at Cassio's legs, and hurries off.*

CASSIO   I am maimed for ever. Help, ho! Murder! Murder!
                          [*He falls.*

Enter OTHELLO.

OTHELLO   The voice of Cassio: Iago keeps his word.
RODERIGO   O, villain that I am!
OTHELLO   It is even so.
CASSIO   O, help, ho! Light! A surgeon!   30
OTHELLO   'Tis he. O brave Iago, honest and just,
           That hast such noble sense of thy friend's wrong,
           Thou teachest me. Minion, your dear lies dead,
           And your unblest fate hies: strumpet, I come.
           Forth of my heart, those charms, thine eyes, are blotted;
           Thy bed, lust-stained, shall with lust's blood be spotted.
                                                      [*Exit.*

Enter LODOVICO *and* GRATIANO.

CASSIO   What, ho! No watch? No passage? Murder! Murder!
GRATIANO   'Tis some mischance; the voice is very direful.
CASSIO   O, help!
LODOVICO   Hark!   40
RODERIGO   O wretched villain!
LODOVICO   Two or three groan. It is a heavy night;
           These may be counterfeits: let's think't unsafe
           To come in to the cry without more help.
                                          [*They stand aside.*

RODERIGO   Nobody come? Then shall I bleed to death.
LODOVICO   Hark!

Enter IAGO *with a light.*

GRATIANO   Here's one comes in his shirt, with light and weapons.
IAGO   Who's there? Whose noise is this that cries on murder?
LODOVICO   We do not know.
IAGO   Did not you hear a cry?
CASSIO   Here, here! For heaven's sake, help me!
IAGO   What's the matter? 50
GRATIANO   This is Othello's ancient, as I take it.
LODOVICO   The same indeed; a very valiant fellow.
IAGO   [*to Cassio:*] What are you here that cry so grievously?
CASSIO   Iago? O, I am spoiled, undone by villains!
           Give me some help.
IAGO   O me, lieutenant! What villains have done this?
CASSIO   I think that one of them is hereabout,

And cannot make away.

IAGO   O treacherous villains!
[*to Lodovico and Gratiano:*]
What are you there? Come in and give some help.

RODERIGO O, help me here!   60

CASSIO   That's one of them.

IAGO   O murderous slave! O villain!
                              [*He stabs Roderigo.*

RODERIGO O damned Iago! O inhuman dog!

IAGO   Kill men i'th'dark! Where be these bloody thieves?
         How silent is this town! Ho! Murder, murder!
                   [*Lodovico and Gratiano come forward.*
         What may you be? Are you of good or evil?

LODOVICO As you shall prove us, praise us.

IAGO   Signior Lodovico?

LODOVICO He, sir.

IAGO   I cry you mercy. Here's Cassio hurt by villains.

GRATIANO Cassio?   70

IAGO   How is't, brother?

CASSIO   My leg is cut in two.

IAGO   Marry, heaven forbid!
         Light, gentlemen: I'll bind it with my shirt.

                    Enter BIANCA.

BIANCA   What is the matter, ho? Who is't that cried?

IAGO   [*in mimicry:*] 'Who is't that cried?'

BIANCA   O my dear Cassio!
         My sweet Cassio! O Cassio, Cassio, Cassio!

IAGO   O notable strumpet! Cassio, may you suspect
         Who they should be, that have thus mangled you?

CASSIO   No.

GRATIANO I am sorry to find you thus; I have been to seek you.   80

IAGO   Lend me a garter. So. – O for a chair,
         To bear him easily hence![153]

BIANCA   Alas, he faints! O Cassio, Cassio, Cassio!

IAGO   Gentlemen all, I do suspect this trash
         To be a party in this injury.
         Patience awhile, good Cassio. Come, come;
         Lend me a light. [*He turns to Roderigo.*] Know we
                                   this face or no?

	Alas, my friend and my dear countryman
	Roderigo? No – yes, sure; O heaven, Roderigo.
GRATIANO	What, of Venice?

IAGO   Even he, sir. Did you know him?

GRATIANO   Know him? Ay.

IAGO   Signior Gratiano? I cry your gentle pardon:
These bloody accidents must excuse my manners,
That so neglected you.

GRATIANO   I am glad to see you.

IAGO   How do you, Cassio? O, a chair, a chair!

GRATIANO Roderigo!

IAGO   He, he, 'tis he. [*A chair is brought.*] O, that's well said;
                                        the chair.
Some good man bear him carefully from hence;
I'll fetch the general's surgeon. [*To Bianca:*] For you,
                                        mistress,
Save you your labour. [*To Cassio:*] He that lies
                              slain here, Cassio,

Was my dear friend. What malice was between you?

CASSIO   None in the world; nor do I know the man.

IAGO   [*to Bianca:*]
What, look you pale? – O, bear him out o'th'air.

                              [*Cassio is carried off.*
Stay you, good gentlemen. – Look you pale, mistress?
– Do you perceive the gastness of her eye? –
Nay, if you stare, we shall hear more anon.
– Behold her well; I pray you, look upon her:
Do you see, gentlemen? Nay, guiltiness will speak,
Though tongues were out of use.

                    Enter EMILIA.

EMILIA   'Las, what's the matter? What's the matter, husband?

IAGO   Cassio hath here been set on in the dark
By Roderigo and fellows that are scaped:
He's almost slain, and Roderigo dead.

EMILIA   Alas, good gentleman! Alas, good Cassio!

IAGO   This is the fruits of whoring. Prithee, Emilia,
Go know of Cassio where he supped tonight.
[*To Bianca:*] What, do you shake at that?

BIANCA   He supped at my house, but I therefore shake not.

IAGO   O, did he so? I charge you, go with me.
EMILIA O, fie upon thee, strumpet!   120
BIANCA I am no strumpet, but of life as honest
        As you that thus abuse me.
EMILIA   As I? Foh! Fie upon thee!
IAGO   Kind gentlemen, let's go see poor Cassio dressed.
        – Come, mistress, you must tell's another tale. –
        Emilia, run you to the citadel,
        And tell my lord and lady what hath happed.
        Will you go on afore? [*Aside:*] This is the night
        That either makes me or fordoes me quite.   [*Exeunt.*

SCENE 2.

A chamber in the citadel; DESDEMONA *lies asleep in bed.*

Enter OTHELLO *with a light.*

OTHELLO It is the cause, it is the cause, my soul.
        Let me not name it to you, you chaste stars;
        It is the cause.[154] Yet I'll not shed her blood,
        Nor scar that whiter skin of hers than snow
        And smooth as monumental alabaster;
        Yet she must die, else she'll betray more men.
        Put out the light, and then put out the light.[155]
        If I quench thee, thou flaming minister,
        I can again thy former light restore
        Should I repent me; but once put out thy light,   10
        Thou cunning'st pattern of excelling nature,
        I know not where is that Promethean heat
        That can thy light relume.[156] When I have plucked
                                        the rose,
        I cannot give it vital growth again:
        It needs must wither. I'll smell it on the tree.
        [*He kisses her.*] O balmy breath, that dost almost
                                        persuade
        Justice to break her sword![157] One more, one more.
        Be thus when thou art dead, and I will kill thee
        And love thee after. One more, and that's the last.
        [*He kisses her.*] So sweet was ne'er so fatal. I must weep, 20

But they are cruel tears; this sorrow's heavenly:
It strikes where it doth love.[158] She wakes.

DESDEM.   Who's there? Othello?

OTHELLO   Ay, Desdemona.

DESDEM.   Will you come to bed, my lord?

OTHELLO   Have you prayed tonight, Desdemona?

DESDEM.   Ay, my lord.

OTHELLO   If you bethink yourself of any crime
Unreconciled as yet to heaven and grace,
Solicit for it straight.

DESDEM.   Alack, my lord, what may you mean by that?   30

OTHELLO   Well, do it, and be brief; I will walk by.
I would not kill thy unpreparèd spirit;
No – heaven forfend! – I would not kill thy soul.[159]

DESDEM.   Talk you of killing?

OTHELLO   Ay, I do.

DESDEM.   Then heaven
Have mercy on me!

OTHELLO   Amen, with all my heart!

DESDEM.   If you say so, I hope you will not kill me.

OTHELLO   Hum!

DESDEM.   And yet I fear you; for you're fatal then
When your eyes roll so. Why I should fear I know not,
Since guiltiness I know not; but yet I feel I fear.   40

OTHELLO   Think on thy sins.

DESDEM.   They are loves I bear to you.

OTHELLO   Ay, and for that thou diest.[160]

DESDEM.   That death's unnatural that kills for loving.
Alas, why gnaw you so your nether lip?
Some bloody passion shakes your very frame:
These are porténts; but yet I hope, I hope,
They do not point on me.

OTHELLO   Peace, and be still!

DESDEM.   I will, so. What's the matter?

OTHELLO   That handkerchief which I so loved and gave thee,
Thou gav'st to Cassio.

DESDEM.   No, by my life and soul!   50
Send for the man, and ask him.

OTHELLO   Sweet soul, take heed,

        Take heed of perjury: thou art on thy death-bed.

DESDEM.   Ay, but not yet to die.

OTHELLO   Yes, presently;
        Therefore confess thee freely of thy sin;
        For to deny each article with oath
        Cannot remove nor choke the strong conception
        That I do groan withal. Thou art to die.

DESDEM.   Then Lord have mercy on me!

OTHELLO   I say, amen.

DESDEM.   And have you mercy too! I never did
        Offend you in my life; never loved Cassio,   60
        But with such general warranty of heaven
        As I might love. I never gave him token.

OTHELLO   By heaven, I saw my handkerchief in's hand!
        O perjured woman, thou dost stone my heart,[161]
        And mak'st me call what I intend to do
        A murder, which I thought a sacrifice.
        I saw the handkerchief.

DESDEM.   He found it, then;
        I never gave it him. Send for him hither:
        Let him confess a truth.

OTHELLO   He hath confessed.

DESDEM   What, my lord?   70

OTHELLO   That he hath used thee.

DESDEM.   How? Unlawfully?

OTHELLO   Ay.

DESDEM.   He will not say so.

OTHELLO   No, his mouth is stopped;
        Honest Iago hath ta'en order for't.

DESDEM.   O, my fear interprets! What, is he dead?

OTHELLO   Had all his hairs been lives, my great revenge
        Had stomach for them all.

DESDEM.   Alas, he is betrayed, and I undone![162]

OTHELLO   Out, strumpet! Weep'st thou for him to my face?

DESDEM.   O, banish me, my lord, but kill me not!

OTHELLO   Down, strumpet!   80

DESDEM.   Kill me tomorrow; let me live tonight!

OTHELLO   Nay, if you strive —

DESDEM.	But half an hour!
OTHELLO	Being done, there is no pause.[163]
DESDEM.	But while I say one prayer!
OTHELLO	It is too late.
DESDEM.	O Lord, Lord, Lord – [He smothers her.[164]
EMILIA	[beyond the door:] My lord, my lord! What, ho! My lord, my lord!
OTHELLO	What noise is this? – Not dead? Not yet quite dead? I that am cruel am yet merciful; I would not have thee linger in thy pain. So, so. [He repeats the smothering.
EMILIA	[outside:] What, ho! My lord, my lord!
OTHELLO	Who's there? 90
EMILIA	[outside:] O, good my lord, I'd speak a word with you!
OTHELLO	Yes: 'tis Emilia. – By and by. – She's dead. 'Tis like she comes to speak of Cassio's death: The noise was high. Ha! No more moving? Still as the grave. Shall she come in? Were't good? I think she stirs again. No. What's best to do? If she come in, she'll sure speak to my wife – My wife, my wife: what wife? I have no wife. O insupportable! O heavy hour! Methinks it should be now a huge eclipse 100 Of sun and moon, and that th'affrighted globe Should yawn at alteration.[165]
EMILIA	[outside:] I do beseech you That I may speak with you. O, good my lord!
OTHELLO	I had forgot thee: O, come in, Emilia. Soft, by and by; let me the curtains draw. Where art thou? [He opens the door.

Enter EMILIA.

	What's the matter with thee now?
EMILIA	O, my good lord, yonder's foul murder done!
OTHELLO	What, now?
EMILIA	But now, my lord.
OTHELLO	It is the very error of the moon; 110 She comes more nearer earth than she was wont And makes men mad.
EMILIA	Cassio, my lord, hath killed a young Venetian

Called Roderigo.

OTHELLO   Roderigo killed,
And Cassio killed?

EMILIA   No, Cassio is not killed.

OTHELLO Not Cassio killed! Then murder's out of tune,
And sweet revenge grows harsh.

DESDEM. O, falsely, falsely murdered!

EMILIA   O Lord, what cry is that?

OTHELLO That? What?

EMILIA Out, and alas! That was my lady's voice.   120

                    [*She opens the bed-curtains.*

Help! Help, ho! Help! O lady, speak again!
Sweet Desdemona! O sweet mistress, speak!

DESDEM. A guiltless death I die.

EMILIA   O, who hath done
This deed?

DESDEM.   Nobody; I myself. Farewell;
Commend me to my kind lord: O, farewell![166] [*She dies.*

OTHELLO Why, how should she be murdered?

EMILIA   Alas, who knows?

OTHELLO You heard her say herself, it was not I.

EMILIA She said so: I must needs report the truth.

OTHELLO She's like a liar gone to burning hell:
'Twas I that killed her.

EMILIA   O, the more angel she,   130
And you the blacker devil!

OTHELLO She turned to folly, and she was a whore.

EMILIA Thou dost belie her, and thou art a devil.

OTHELLO She was false as water.

EMILIA   Thou art rash as fire to say
That she was false: O, she was heavenly true!

OTHELLO Cassio did top her: ask thy husband else.
O, I were damned beneath all depth in hell,
But that I did proceed upon just grounds
To this extremity. Thy husband knew it all.

EMILIA My husband?   140

OTHELLO Thy husband.

EMILIA That she was false to wedlock?

OTHELLO Ay, with Cassio. Nay, had she been true,

> If heaven would make me such another world
> Of one entire and perfect chrysolite,
> I'd not have sold her for it.

EMILIA   My husband?

OTHELLO   Ay, 'twas he that told me first;
> An honest man he is, and hates the slime
> That sticks on filthy deeds.

EMILIA   My husband?   150

OTHELLO   What needs this iterance, woman? I say thy husband.

EMILIA   O mistress, villainy hath made mocks with love!
> My husband say that she was false?

OTHELLO   He, woman;
> I say thy husband: dost understand the word?
> My friend, thy husband, honest, honest Iago.[167]

EMILIA   If he say so, may his pernicious soul
> Rot half a grain a day! He lies to th'heart.
> She was too fond of her most filthy bargain.

OTHELLO   [drawing his sword:] Ha?

EMILIA   Do thy worst.   160
> This deed of thine is no more worthy heaven
> Than thou wast worthy her.

OTHELLO   Peace, you were best.

EMILIA   Thou hast not half that power to do me harm
> As I have to be hurt. O gull, O dolt,
> As ignorant as dirt! Thou hast done a deed –
> I care not for thy sword; I'll make thee known,
> Though I lost twenty lives. Help! Help, ho! Help!
> The Moor hath killed my mistress! Murder! Murder!

Enter MONTANO, GRATIANO, IAGO *and* OTHERS.

MONTANO   What is the matter? How now, general?

EMILIA   O, are you come, Iago? You have done well,   170
> That men must lay their murders on your neck.

GRATIANO   What is the matter?

EMILIA   [to Iago:] Disprove this villain, if thou be'st a man.
> He says thou told'st him that his wife was false.
> I know thou didst not: thou'rt not such a villain.
> Speak, for my heart is full.

IAGO   I told him what I thought, and told no more

Than what he found himself was apt and true.

EMILIA But did you ever tell him she was false?

IAGO I did.

EMILIA You told a lie, an odious, damnèd lie;
Upon my soul, a lie, a wicked lie!
She false with Cassio! Did you say with Cassio?

IAGO With Cassio, mistress. Go to, charm your tongue.

EMILIA I will not charm my tongue; I am bound to speak:
My mistress here lies murdered in her bed –

ALL O heavens forfend!

EMILIA And your reports have set the murder on.

OTHELLO Nay, stare not, masters: it is true indeed.

GRATIANO 'Tis a strange truth.

MONTANO O monstrous act!

EMILIA Villainy, villainy, villainy!
I think upon't; I think: I smell't: O villainy!
I thought so then; I'll kill myself for grief.
O villainy, villainy![168]

IAGO What, are you mad? I charge you, get you home.

EMILIA Good gentlemen, let me have leave to speak:
'Tis proper I obey him, but not now.
– Perchance, Iago, I will ne'er go home.

OTHELLO O! O! O! [*Othello falls on the bed*

EMILIA Nay, lay thee down and roar;
For thou hast killed the sweetest innocent
That e'er did lift up eye.

OTHELLO [*rising:*] O, she was foul!
I scarce did know you, uncle. There lies your niece,
Whose breath indeed these hands have newly stopped.
I know this act shows horrible and grim.

GRATIANO Poor Desdemon! I am glad thy father's dead.
Thy match was mortal to him, and pure grief
Shore his old thread in twain.[169] Did he live now,
This sight would make him do a desperate turn,
Yea, curse his better angel from his side,
And fall to reprobance.

OTHELLO 'Tis pitiful; but yet Iago knows
That she with Cassio hath the act of shame
A thousand times committed. Cassio confessed it;

And she did gratify his amorous works
With that recognizance and pledge of love
Which I first gave her — I saw it in his hand:
It was a handkerchief, an antique token
My father gave my mother.

EMILIA   O God, O heavenly God!

IAGO   Zounds! Hold your peace.

EMILIA   'Twill out, 'twill out. I peace?
No, I will speak as liberal as the north;[170]   220
Let heaven and men and devils, let them all,
All, all, cry shame against me, yet I'll speak.

IAGO   Be wise, and get you home.

EMILIA   I will not.

            [*Iago threatens her with his sword.*

GRATIANO   Fie!
Your sword upon a woman?

EMILIA   O thou dull Moor! That handkerchief thou speak'st of,
I found by fortune and did give my husband:
For often with a solemn earnestness
(More than indeed belonged to such a trifle)
He begged of me to steal it.

IAGO   Villainous whore!

EMILIA   She give it Cassio? No, alas, I found it,   230
And I did give't my husband.

IAGO   Filth, thou liest.

EMILIA   By heaven, I do not, I do not, gentlemen.
O murderous coxcomb! What should such a fool
Do with so good a wife?

OTHELLO   Are there no stones in heaven
But what serve for the thunder? Precious villain!

            [*He lunges with a sword at Iago, but Montano disarms him.*
                        Iago wounds Emilia and escapes.

GRATIANO The woman falls; sure, he hath killed his wife.

EMILIA   Ay, ay. O, lay me by my mistress' side.

GRATIANO He's gone, but his wife's killed.

MONTANO   'Tis a notorious villain. Take you this weapon,
Which I have here recovered from the Moor.   240
Come, guard the door without; let him not pass,
But kill him rather. I'll after that same villain,

For 'tis a damnèd slave.

                       [Exeunt all but Othello and Emilia.

OTHELLO   I am not valiant neither,
But every puny whipster gets my sword.
But why should honour outlive honesty?
Let it go all.

EMILIA   What did thy song bode, lady?
Hark, canst thou hear me? I will play the swan,
And die in music. [*She sings:*] 'Willow, willow, willow.'[171]
Moor, she was chaste; she loved thee, cruel Moor;
So come my soul to bliss, as I speak true;   250
So speaking as I think, alas, I die.   [*She dies.*

OTHELLO I have another weapon in this chamber:
It was a sword of Spain, the ice-brook's temper —
O, here it is. — Uncle, I must come forth.

GRATIANO [*at the door:*] If thou attempt it, it will cost thee dear:
Thou hast no weapon, and perforce must suffer.

OTHELLO Look in upon me then, and speak with me,
Or, naked as I am, I will assault thee.

                  Enter GRATIANO.

GRATIANO What is the matter?

OTHELLO   Behold, I have a weapon:
A better never did itself sustain   260
Upon a soldier's thigh. I have seen the day
That with this little arm and this good sword
I have made my way through more impediments
Than twenty times your stop: but (O vain boast!
Who can control his fate?) 'tis not so now.
Be not afraid, though you do see me weaponed:
Here is my journey's end, here is my butt
And very sea-mark of my utmost sail.
Do you go back dismayed? 'Tis a lost fear:
Man but a rush against Othello's breast,   270
And he retires. Where should Othello go?
Now, [*to Desdemona:*] how dost thou look now? O
                        ill-starred wench,[172]
Pale as thy smock. When we shall meet at compt,
This look of thine will hurl my soul from heaven,
And fiends will snatch at it. Cold, cold, my girl?

Even like thy chastity.[173]
O cursèd, cursèd slave! Whip me, ye devils,
From the possession of this heavenly sight!
Blow me about in winds, roast me in sulphur,
Wash me in steep-down gulfs of liquid fire!   280
O Desdemon! Dead Desdemon: dead! O, O!

Enter LODOVICO, MONTANO, CASSIO *carried in a chair, and*
OFFICERS *with the captured* IAGO.

LODOVICO Where is this rash and most unfortunate man?
OTHELLO   That's he that was Othello: here I am.
LODOVICO Where is that viper? Bring the villain forth.
OTHELLO   I look down towards his feet; but that's a fable.[174]
          — If that thou be'st a devil, I cannot kill thee.

                                        [*He wounds Iago.*
LODOVICO Wrench his sword from him.   [*They seize the sword.*
IAGO   I bleed, sir, but not killed.
OTHELLO   I am not sorry neither: I'd have thee live;
          For, in my sense, 'tis happiness to die.
LODOVICO O thou Othello, that wert once so good,   290
          Fall'n in the practice of a damnèd slave,
          What should be said to thee?
OTHELLO   Why, anything:
          An honourable murderer, if you will;
          For nought did I in hate, but all in honour.
LODOVICO This wretch hath part confessed his villainy.
          Did you and he consent in Cassio's death?
OTHELLO   Ay.
CASSIO   Dear general, I never gave you cause.
OTHELLO   I do believe it, and I ask your pardon.
          Will you, I pray, demand that demi-devil   300
          Why he hath thus ensnared my soul and body?
IAGO   Demand me nothing: what you know, you know;
          From this time forth, I never will speak word.
LODOVICO What, not to pray?
GRATIANO   Torments will ope your lips.
OTHELLO   Well, thou dost best.
LODOVICO Sir, you shall understand what hath befall'n,
          Which, as I think, you know not. Here is a letter,
          Found in the pocket of the slain Roderigo,

       And here another: the one of them imports
       The death of Cassio to be undertook   310
       By Roderigo.
OTHELLO O villain!
CASSIO   Most heathenish and most gross!
LODOVICO Now here's another discontented paper,
       Found in his pocket too: and this, it seems,
       Roderigo meant t'have sent this damnèd villain;
       But that, belike, Iago in the nick
       Came in and satisfied him.
OTHELLO   O the pernicious caitiff!
       How came you, Cassio, by that handkerchief
       That was my wife's?
CASSIO   I found it in my chamber:
       And he himself confessed but even now   320
       That there he dropped it for a special purpose
       Which wrought to his desire.
OTHELLO   O fool, fool, fool!
CASSIO There is besides, in Roderigo's letter,
       How he upbraids Iago that he made him
       Brave me upon the watch, whereon it came
       That I was cast; and even but now he spake
       (After long seeming dead) Iago hurt him,
       Iago set him on.
LODOVICO [to Othello:] You must forsake this room, and go with us;
       Your power and your command is taken off,   330
       And Cassio rules in Cyprus. For this slave,
       If there be any cunning cruelty
       That can torment him much and hold him long,
       It shall be his. You shall close prisoner rest,
       Till that the nature of your fault be known
       To the Venetian state. Come, bring away.
OTHELLO Soft you; a word or two before you go.
       I have done the state some service, and they know't.
       No more of that. I pray you, in your letters,
       When you shall these unlucky deeds relate,   340
       Speak of me as I am: nothing extenuate,
       Nor set down aught in malice. Then must you speak
       Of one that loved not wisely but too well;

Of one not easily jealous, but, being wrought,
Perplexed in the extreme; of one whose hand,
Like the base Indian,[175] threw a pearl away
Richer than all his tribe; of one whose subdued eyes,
Albeit unusèd to the melting mood,
Drops tears as fast as the Arabian trees
Their med'cinable gum.[176] Set you down this;   350
And say besides, that in Aleppo once,
Where a malignant and a turbaned Turk
Beat a Venetian and traduced the state,
I took by th'throat the circumcisèd dog,
And smote him – thus![177]   [*He stabs himself.*

LODOVICO O bloody period!
GRATIANO   All that's spoke is marred.
OTHELLO [*to Desdemona:*] I kissed thee ere I killed thee; no
                                        way but this:
Killing myself, to die upon a kiss.
                    [*He kisses Desdemona and dies.*
CASSIO   This did I fear (but thought he had no weapon),
For he was great of heart.
LODOVICO [*to Iago:*]   O Spartan dog,[178]   360
More fell than anguish, hunger, or the sea,
Look on the tragic loading of this bed:
This is thy work. The object poisons sight;
Let it be hid. [*They close the curtains.*] Gratiano, keep
                                        the house,
And seize upon the fortunes of the Moor,
For they succeed on you. [*To Cassio:*] To you,
                    - lord governor,
Remains the censure of this hellish villain,
The time, the place, the torture: O, enforce it!
Myself will straight aboard, and to the state
This heavy act with heavy heart relate.   370
                                        [*Exeunt.*

NOTES ON *OTHELLO*

In these notes, the abbreviations used include the following:

EH: *Othello*, ed. E. A. J. Honigmann (Walton-on Thames: Nelson, 1997).

F1:   First Folio, 1623.

F2:   Second Folio, 1632.

HN: Gaius Plinius Secundus (Pliny the Elder): *The Historie of the World. Commonly Called, The Naturall Historie.* Translated by Philemon Holland. London: 1601.

i.e.:   *id est* (that is).

O.E.D.: *The Oxford English Dictionary.*

Q1:   First Quarto, 1621.

Q2:   Second Quarto, 1630.

S.D.:   stage direction.

Biblical quotations are from the Geneva Bible (1560).

In the case of a pun or an ambiguity, the meanings are distinguished as (a) and (b), or as (a), (b) and (c).

1 (1.1. S.D.) *IAGO*:   The name may recall Santiago Matamoros, St. James the Moor-Slayer, the patron saint of Spain. (Iago's counterpart in the source-tale is not named.) In *Othello*, 'Iago' is usually trisyllabic.

2 (1.1.4) *'Sblood*:   This oath ('By God's blood') is present in Q1 but absent from F1: the first of many instances in which words which might be deemed profane have either been deleted from the F1 text or have been moderated there. (This was probably in

response to the 'Acte to Restraine Abuses of Players', 1606.) F1
deletes 'God' from line 33 and 'Zounds' from lines 86 and 108.

3 (1.1.21) *A fellow . . . wife*: The line may be corrupt. It is
unclear why anyone should be 'almost damned' by having a fair
wife (or be 'damned' by 'almost' having one), and Cassio is
subsequently depicted as a bachelor. In the source-tale by
Cinthio, the counterpart to Cassio is a married man: so
Shakespeare may have adopted this detail but subsequently
changed his mind.

4 (1.1.24–6) *unless . . . as he*: 'unless you count knowledge of
mere academic theory, a matter which gowned councillors can
propound as impressively as he'. Q1 has 'toged'; F1 has
'tongued'; either makes sense.

5 (1.1.30–31) *must . . . creditor*: 'must have the wind taken out
of my sails by a mere accountant'.

6 (1.1.33) *His . . . ancient*: An 'ancient' or ensign is a standard-
bearer; 'regimental sergeant-major' would be an approximate
modern equivalent. (Q1 has 'Ancient'; F1 has 'Auntient'.)
Meanwhile, Cassio has become no ordinary lieutenant: he is
now Othello's 'own second' (2.3.126): his second-in-command.
'Moorship's' is Iago's mocking variant on 'Worship's'. (Q1 has
'Worships', but F1 has 'Mooreships'.)

7 (1.1.57) *Were . . . Iago*: 'if I were Othello, his employee
would not be Iago (for I would not be so foolish as to employ
a selfish hypocrite)'.

8 (1.1.60–63) *for my . . . extern*: 'for my particular purpose,
because when my overt conduct manifests the inner activity
and plan of my desires in a complementary display,'.

9 (1.1.68) *Rouse . . . delight*: perhaps: 'rouse Brabantio, pursue
Othello, poison Othello's delight'.

10 (1.1.72–3) *Yet . . . colour*: 'nevertheless cast such varied annoy-
ances on it that it may be weakened [or that it may lose some
reason for its existence]'. Q1 has 'changes'; F1 has 'chances'.

11 (1.1.76–7) *As . . . cities*: 'as when, in populous cities, a fire is
perceived at night by people who had negligently overlooked
its inception'.

12 (1.1.116) *making . . . backs*: copulating in a conventional position.

13 (1.1.120–36) *If't be . . . everywhere*:   These lines, present in F1,
are absent from Q1. Probably they were cut from the script
used for Q1.

14 (1.1.148–49) *he's embarked . . . wars*:   'he's committed, by such
vehement persuasion, to the war involving Cyprus'. Ottoman
Turks, seeking to conquer the Venetian island of Cyprus, were
repulsed at the Battle of Lepanto, 1571, when the Muslim fleet
was vanquished by the Christian fleet, but gained Cyprus in
1573. (In *Othello*, the destruction of the Turkish vessels by a
storm recalls the destruction of the Spanish Armada in 1588.)

15 (1.1.152) *business*:   here trisyllabic ('busyness'), so that the line
is a regular iambic pentameter. (Compare 'action' in 2.3.128.)

16 (1.1.157) *Lead . . . search*:   'lead the aroused search party to the
Sagittary'. The Sagittary would be an inn with the sign of
Sagittarius, the centaur.

17 (1.2.5) *yerked . . . ribs*:   'stabbed him in this place, under the
ribs'. F1 has 'yerk'd' ('struck'); Q1 has 'ierk'd' ('jerked'). The
'him' may be Brabantio but is probably Roderigo.

18 (1.2.21) *promúlgate*:   'make publicly known'. F1 has 'promulgate'; Q1 has 'provulgate', which means much the same.

19 (1.2.25) *Desdemona*:   The name means 'the unfortunate
female'. The source tale by Cinthio refers to 'Disdemona' as
'unfortunate', and says that 'her father . . . had given her a name
of unlucky augury'.

20 (1.2.32–3) *Is . . . no*:   Othello's question, coupled with later
indications (e.g. at 3.3.38), suggests that he may be short-
sighted, a detail with thematic import. It is also appropriate that
Iago swears by Janus, the two-faced god.

21 (1.2.63) *Damned . . . her*:   Devils were thought to be black, so
Brabantio associates Othello with the powers of a devil who
can wield black magic.

22 (1.2.65) *If . . . bound*:   This line is absent from Q1 but present
in F1.

23 (1.2.72–7) *Judge . . . thee*:   These line are absent from Q1
(having probably been cut), but are present in F1. Q1 begins
the next line with 'Such' instead of 'For'.

24 (1.3.10–12): *I do . . . sense*:   'I do not seek reassurance from the
variation, but rather assent in trepidation to the main point'.

25 (1.3.24–30) *For that . . . profitless*:   Q1 lacks these lines.

26 (1.3.36) SENATOR *. . . guess?*:   This line is absent from Q1 but
present in F1, as is line 63 later.

27 (1.3.42) *believe him*:   Both Q1 and F1 have 'beleeue him'.
Some editors change this to 'relieve him', as Montano (at
2.1.30) is glad that Othello arrives to take command.

28 (1.3.67–70) *the bloody . . . action*:   'you yourself shall, according to your interpretation, pronounce the stern sentence from
the book of severe legal penalties'.

29 (1.3.91–4) *what drugs . . . daughter*:   To insert 'with' before
'what drugs' would improve the grammar but mar the metre.

30 (1.3.118) *The trust . . . you*:   This line is absent from Q1 but
present in F1.

31 (1.3.129–45) *the story . . . shoulders*:   Othello's life-story derives in part from that of John Leo (Leo Africanus), as described
by John Pory in his translation (1600) of Leo's *A Geographical
Historie of Africa*. Leo, a cultured, much-travelled warrior and
scholar, was captured by pirates and taken to Rome. Pory says:
'I marvell much how euer he should haue escaped so manie
thousands of imminent dangers . . . For how many desolate
cold mountaines, and huge drie, and barren deserts passed he?'
Some descriptive details may derive from Pliny's *Historia
Naturalis*. Pliny refers to cannibalistic Scythians 'called
Anthropophagi', and says that in India 'some there bee without
heads standing upon their neckes, who carrie eies in their
shoulders' (*HN*, pp. 153, 154, 156). EH, p. 6, reproduces an
illustration from Sebastian Munster's *Cosmographia* (1572)
which shows a man whose face is incorporated in his chest.

32 (1.3.159) *sighs*:   F1 has 'kisses'.

33 (1.3.163) *made . . . man*:   (a) 'made such a man for her as a
potential husband'; (b) 'created her as a man like that'.

34 (1.3.194) *Which . . . heart*:   This line is absent from Q1 but
present in F1.

35 (1.3.199) *like yourself*:   (a) 'in your style, by offering general
reflections on this matter'; (b) 'in the manner of your better self'.

36 (1.3.203) *which . . . depended*: 'which until recently had been subject to (and concealed by) our hopes'.

37 (1.3.212–13) *He . . . hears*: 'A man accepts the judicial sentence well if he brings away nothing but the cost-free consolation which he hears'.

38 (1.3.219) *That . . . ear*: 'that the wounded heart was (consolingly) penetrated by words'. Q1 has 'pierced'; F1 has 'pieced'. Some editors prefer the latter, taking it to mean 'mended'.

39 (1.3.239–40) *If . . . father's*: Q1 has: 'If you please, bee't at her fathers'. F1 has: 'Why at her Fathers?'

40 (1.3.249) *My . . . fortunes*: 'my forthright violation and defiance of my prospects'.

41 (1.3.250–51) *subdued . . . lord*: 'subordinated completely to the true character of my lord'. Q1 has 'vtmost pleasure of my Lord'; F1 has 'very quality of my Lord'.

42 (1.3.263–4) *Nor . . . satisfaction*: 'nor to satisfy sexual ardour (my youthful lusts being now defunct) and gain personal gratification'. Q1 has: 'Nor to comply with heate, the young affects / In my defunct, and proper satisfaction'; F1 is similar. The phrasing may be corrupt.

43 (1.3.277–8) *And speed . . . heart*: I follow Q1's version. F1 has: 'And speed must answer it. / Sen. You must away to night. / Othe. With all my heart.'

44 (1.3.292–3) *Look . . . thee*: an idea that Iago will amplify.

45 (1.3.322) *tine*: Q1 and F1 have 'Time', so some editors prefer 'thyme' here; but, as thyme is a pleasant herb, whereas tine is the wild vetch or tare, tine is what would be weeded up.

46 (1.3.338–9) *defeat . . . beard*: (a) 'disguise your face with a false beard'; (b) 'overcome your (youthful) appearance by wearing a false beard'.

47 (1.3.356–7) *hanged . . . joy*: 'hanged for achieving your pleasure'. (Perhaps the hanging is to be understood as a punishment for rape.)

48 (1.3.377) *I'll . . . land*: F1 has 'Ile sell all my land'; Q1 lacks this statement. F1, however, lacks the Q1 lines given here as 373–6.

49 (2.1.26) *A Veronesa*:   probably 'a ship made in or provided by
Verona'. Although Verona is an inland city, ships were made
there on the navigable river Adige; and some could have been
provided or manned by the Veronese, who were Venetian
subjects. (Vessels supplied by Verona fought in the Battle of
Lepanto.)

50 (2.1.39–40) *Even . . . regard*:   These words are absent from Q1
but present in F1.

51 (2.1.51–4) *A sail . . . A sail!*':   Q1 ascribes to 'a Messenger' not
only the words 'A saile, a saile, a saile.' but also the reply to
Cassio's question. F1 gives the former words to a voice '*Within*'
and the latter to an unspecified gentleman.

52 (2.1.64–5) *And in . . . ingener*:   (a) 'and her natural beauty
exhausts the poet's capacity to invent praise'; (b) 'and in the
manifestation of her very essence (her soul) exhausts the
creativity of the divine inventor, God (so that she will never be
surpassed)'. Q1 has 'And in the essentiall vesture of creation, /
Does beare all excellency'; F1 has 'And in th'essentiall Vesture
of Creation, / Do's tyre the Ingeniuer'.

53 (2.1.107–8) *She . . . thinking*:   'instead of using her tongue to
rebuke me, she harbours hostile emotions and chides me
mentally'.

54 (2.1.112–13) *Players . . . beds*:   (a) 'merely playing about when
you should be prudent housewives, but rationing (like parsi-
monious housewives) your favours in bed'; (b) 'merely playing
about when you should be prudent housewives, but being
promiscuous hussies in your sexual lives'.

55 (2.1.125–6) *my invention . . . frieze*:   'my imaginative ideas
come from my head as birdlime does from hairy cloth' (i.e.,
with great difficulty). 'Birdlime' is a sticky paste smeared on
branches to ensnare birds, and 'frieze' is a coarse cloth with a
raised nap.

56 (2.1.125–8) *I am . . . delivered*:   Though set as poetry here,
these lines hover aurally between poetry (as in Q1) and prose
(as in F1).

57 (2.1.132–33) *If she . . . hit*:   'If she is dark-complexioned (or
dark-haired) and also possesses intelligence, she will find a fair-

complexioned (or fair-haired) man who will penetrate her.'
'White' (fair) puns on 'wight' (person), and 'her blackness' may
refer to her genital area.

58 (2.1.154) *To change . . . tail*:   a difficult idiom. One meaning
may be: 'as to exchange her virginity for experience of the
penis' (since 'head' could mean 'maidenhead', and 'tail' could
mean 'penis'). Perhaps the line should be 'To change for the
cod's head the salmon's tail': i.e., 'as to sacrifice for the
worthless penis her valuable virginity'. ('Cod' could also mean
'penis', as in 'codpiece'; 'tail' could also mean 'pudendum'; and
a fish's head is worthless, whereas good flesh can be found near
its tail.) The original line may, however, mean 'as to prefer the
lowest rank (the tail) of the gentry to the head of the
yeomanry'.

59 (2.1.156) *See . . . behind*:   This line is absent from Q1 but
present in F1.

60 (2.1.188) *Succeeds . . . fate*:   'will ensue in our as-yet-unknown
destiny'.

61 (2.1.195–6) *O, you . . . am*:   'Oh, you are in excellent harmony
now; but I shall unwind the pegs that produce this music, for all
my reputed honesty.' To 'set down the pegs' is to slacken the
strings (which are normally wound tight on those pegs, as on a
violin) so as to result in flat and discordant tones.

62 (2.1.237–8) *that . . . itself*:   'who sees how to contrive opportunities even when no real opportunity arises'. 'Stamp' means
'mint (as a coin)'.

63 (2.1.293–6) *Which . . . hip*:   'Concerning this matter to be
done: if this feeble rubbishy Venetian, whom I keep hungry so
that he will be a keener hunter, responds to my instigation, I'll
take Michael Cassio at a disadvantage'. Q1 has 'crush' where F1
has 'trace'. 'Trace', in hawking, means 'keep hungry'; but the
word may also mean both 'pursue' and 'harness' (so that 'trace
for' can be interpreted as 'harness to prevent'). Some editors
prefer to read 'trash', meaning 'to restrain (a hound)'.

64 (2.3.48–50) *noble . . . isle*:   'fellows of fine proud spirit who,
vigilant in guarding their honour (from disgrace), are the true
essence of this island inured to conflict,'.

65 (2.3. S.D.) GENTLEMEN: Some editions specify also the entry
of servants bearing wine, though Q1 and F1 do not.

66 (2.3.78–85) *King . . . thee*:   'King Stephen was a worthy ruler.
His trousers cost him only five shillings [25 pence], but he still
thought they were sixpence [2½ pence] too costly; so he called
the tailor a rogue. He was a person of high renown, and you are
merely of the lower class. It's pride that ruins the country; so
wrap yourself in (and be satisfied with) your old cloak.' This
ballad was variously known as 'Bell My Wife' and 'Take Thy
Old Cloak about Thee'.

67 (2.3.157–8) *to ourselves . . . Ottomites*:   'destroy ourselves,
when heavenly power (by scattering their fleet) has prevented
the Ottoman Turks from destroying us'.

68 (2.3.169) *As if . . . men*:   It was believed that planets could
make people mad if they came too close to the earth.

69 (2.3.204) *'Tis . . . began't?*:   'Monstrous' could be pronounced
trisyllabically ('monsterous'), regularising the metre.

70 (2.3.205) *If . . . office*:   'If, being biased by allegiance or
because he is a military comrade,'.

71 (2.3.265–7) *Drunk . . . shadow!*:   These words are absent from
Q1 but present in F1.

72 (2.3.327–8) *Even . . . function*:   'even as her sexual desire
commands like a god his submissive capacities'.

73 (2.3.349) *How . . . patience!*:   'Patience' could be pronounced
trisyllabically to maintain the metre.

74 (3.1.3–4) *have . . . thus?*:   Some men who suffered from
venereal disease (known as the 'Neapolitan' disease, because of
the abundance of prostitutes in Naples) had their noses eaten
away by it, marring their speech. The Clown says that the
musical instruments sound similarly 'nasal', out of tune.

75 (3.1.8–10) *thereby . . . know*:   'Thereby hangs a tale' is
proverbial, meaning 'There's a story to be told about that'; but
the Clown exploits the homophone 'tail' (meaning both
'animal's tail' and 'penis') in order to link musical wind
instruments with the anus, which plays the music of flatulence.

76 (3.1.50) *take . . . front*:   The proverbial phrase, 'Take time by
the forelock' (i.e. 'Seize the opportunity'), refers to the classical

figure *Occasio* (Opportunity), who was depicted and described as having long hair over the brow while being bald at the back of the head.

77 (3.3.12–13) *He shall . . . distance*: 'he will keep aloofly at a distance only while it is prudent to do so'.

78 (3.3.14–18) *That policy . . . service*: 'that policy of prudence may endure so long, or be eroded by lack of support (so that it becomes tedious and makes him satisfied with my replacement), or evolve so far from the initial situation, that, while I am absent and someone occupies my place, the general will forget my devotion and past service'. 'Nice and waterish diet' means 'thin and weak nourishment'. (Lines 15–16 are ambiguous, and different editors offer variant interpretations.)

79 (3.3.23) *I'll watch him tame*: a metaphor from falconry: a hawk was kept awake ('watched') to tame it.

80 (3.3.65–8) *And yet . . . check*: 'and yet his transgression, common sense tells us (except that war-time conditions make it necessary to punish the best men as an example), is a fault so slight as to deserve hardly a private reprimand'. Some editors take 'the wars' to mean 'the military profession'.

81 (3.3.91–3) *Excellent . . . again*: 'Excellent creature! May damnation seize my soul if I stop loving you; and, should I ever stop loving you, chaos would return.' Hesiod's *Theogony* says: 'Chaos was born first, and after her came Gaia, . . . Tartaros, . . . and Eros, the fairest of the deathless gods . . . '

82 (3.3.127) *close dilations*: 'private hesitations'. Where F1 has 'dilations', Q1 has 'denotements' (meaning 'indications'). Some editors prefer to emend F1's word as 'delations', meaning both 'accusations' and 'narrations'.

83 (3.3.130–31) *Men . . . none*: 'Men should be as (honest as) they seem; alternatively, if they are not (honest), it's desirable that they may not seem so.'

84 (3.3.140) *I am . . . free to*: 'even slaves are permitted to keep their thoughts to themselves, so I am not obliged to reveal mine.'

85 (3.3.152–4) *that your . . . notice*: Q1 has: 'I intreate you then, / From one that so imperfectly coniects, / You'd take no notice'. F1 has 'that your wisedome / From one, that so imperfectly conceits, / Would take no notice'. Either version would make

sufficient sense. Q1's 'coniects' ('conjects') means 'conjec-
tures'; F1's 'conceits' means 'imagines' or 'speculates'.

86 (3.3.168) OTHELLO ... jealousy: I follow F1 here. In Q1, Iago
says: 'O beware iealousie.'.

87 (3.3.181–2) To follow ... suspicions: 'with that jealousy
repeatedly waxing and waning (like the moon) as new suspicions occur to me'.

88 (3.3.183) Is once ... goat: In Q1, the line appears as: 'Is once
to be resolud: exchange me for a Goate,'. F1 offers: 'Is to be
resolu'd: Exchange me for a Goat,'. (In those texts, 'u' often
serves as a 'v'.) Q1's version is – like some other lines in
Othello – an Alexandrine, having six iambic feet instead of the
customary five; but F1's is awkwardly ambiguous, an irregular
Alexandrine or an irregular pentameter.

89 (3.3.213) To seel ... oak: 'to blind her father's eyes (like those
of a hawk whose eyelids are sewn closed), his lids being as
tightly pressed together as the grain-lines in oak-wood [or
being as tightly shut as the "oak", the outer door of a pair of
doors, which one "sports" – shuts – for privacy]'. Q1 has
'seale', F1 'seele': the former suggests rather the 'sealing' of a
letter with wax; the latter the sewing of the hawk's lids in
course of its taming. Either fits, and neither fits neatly.

90 (3.3.226) As ... friend: Q1 has: 'As my thoughts aime not at:
Cassio's my trusty friend:'. F1 has: 'Which my Thoughts aym'd
not. / Cassio's my worthy Friend:'.

91 (3.3.239–41) Her will ... repent: 'her will, reverting to
her former better standards, may find that you do not match
Italian models of desirability, and she may perhaps (or even
fortunately) repent her choice of you'.

92 (3.3.263–6) If I ... fortune: 'If I find that she is unfaithful,
then, however strong my emotional attachment to her, I will
dismiss her and leave her to fend for herself.' 'Haggard' is a
term for a wild female hawk caught in her adult plumage;
'jesses' are light straps linking a hawk's legs to the leash on a
falconer's wrist; and 'heart-strings' are tendons or nerves
supposed to sustain the heart. The falconer whistles when a
hawk is sent flying; a hawk turned loose is sent downwind; and
'to prey at fortune' means 'to take its chance at finding prey'.

93 (3.3.279–80) *Even . . . quicken*: 'even in the moment of our conception, we are fated to bear eventually the cuckold's horns'.

94 (3.3.305–7) *It is . . . wife*:   He jocularly implies initially that the 'thing' she is offering is her vagina, which he terms 'common': i.e. public, available to anyone. In response to her suspicious 'Ha?', he changes the meaning of 'common thing' to 'everyday occurrence'.

95 (3.3.328) *The Moor . . . poison*:   This line is absent from Q1 but present in F1.

96 (3.3.329–32) *Dangerous . . . sulphur*:   'dangerous ideas are, by nature, poisons which at first hardly taste unpleasant, but, after a little action on the bloodstream, burn like those mines in which sulphur is constantly on fire'. Q1 has 'art' where F1 has 'acte' ('act'): both make sense.

97 (3.3.364) *mine eternal soul*:   Q1 has 'mans eternall soule'; F1 has 'mine eternall Soule'. The former may imply that Iago is imperilling his soul; the latter may imply that Othello is imperilling his own, for he may wrathfully kill Iago.

98 (3.3.379) *That liv'st . . . vice!*:   Q1 has 'liuest', F1 'lou'st'. Iago means that he, Iago, has lived long enough see his honesty deemed a vice or fault.

99 (3.3.389) *Her name*:   F1 has 'My name'; Q2 has 'Her name'.

100 (3.3.386–93) *By the world . . . satisfied!*:   These lines are absent from Q1 but present in F1.

101 (3.3.404) *satisfaction*:   The line is regularised if 'satisfaction' be read as tetrasyllabic (here, though not at line 411).

102 (3.3.432) *'Tis . . . dream*:   Q1 gives this line to Iago, F1 to Othello. The sense is: 'You are shrewdly suspicious, even though this is only a dream.'

103 (3.3.450) *thy hollow cell!*:   Q1 has 'thy hollow Cell,'; F1 has 'the hollow hell,'. Both make sense.

104 (3.3.458–9) *Ne'er . . . Hellespont*:   Here 'feels' follows Q2. F1 has 'keepes' there. The Propontic is the Sea of Marmora (or Marmara), and the Hellespont is the Dardanelles, a strait in north-western Turkey.

105 (3.3.456–63) *Iago . . . heaven*:   After 'Never', these superb lines, present in F1, are absent from Q1.

106 (3.3.471–72) *And . . . ever*.   Q1 has: 'And to obey, shall be remorce, / What bloody worke so euer'; F1 has: 'And to obey shall be in me remorse, / What bloody businesse euer'. To preserve 'in me' would make rather strained sense ('to obey Othello will show my pity for him . . . '). The emendation 'without' fits the next line, which means 'however bloody the action may be'. *O.E.D.* (in its endeavour to make sense of the phrasing here) glosses 'remorse' as 'a solemn obligation'.

107 (3.4.7–8) CLOWN *. . . this?*:   These words are absent from Q1 but present in F1.

108 (3.4.42–3) *The hearts . . . hearts*:   'In former times, love resulted in the giving of hands in marriage; but today's heraldic emblems display hands rather than hearts': i.e., marriage no longer implies faithful love.

109 (3.4.60–62) *my father's . . . fancies*:   Q1 has 'lothely' (i.e. 'loathsome'); F1 has 'loathed'; and 'spirits' (in both Q1 and F1) may be an error for 'spirit'.

110 (3.4.69–70) *A sibyl . . . compasses*:   A sibyl is an enchantress and prophetess who prophesies in a 'fury' or entranced frenzy. The words 'that had numbered in the world / The sun to course two hundred compasses' probably mean 'who was two hundred years old' (as the Cumæan Sibyl was famous for surviving countless years), though AH, p. 339, adopts Samuel Johnson's view that they mean she had predicted that the world would end in two hundred years' time.

111 (3.4.73–4) *dyed . . . hearts*:   'and it was dyed in mummy, which skilful people had processed from the hearts of virgins'. 'Mummy' was a medicinal substance supposedly made from embalmed corpses.

112 (3.4.74) *I'faith, is't true?*:   'I'faith' in Q1 became 'Indeed' in F1, another of the many instances in which religious asseverations were censored or muted. As for the question ('is't true?'), see 5.2.217–18 and *Henry V, War Criminal? and Other Shakespeare Puzzles* by Sutherland and Watts.

113 (3.4.91–2) *I pray . . . handkerchief*.   F1 lacks these words.

114 (3.4.119–20) *shut . . . alms*: 'devote myself to some different course to receive whatever opportunities chance charitably grants me' (i.e., 'I'll trust to luck in a different career').

115 (3.4.123) *in favour . . . altered*: 'as changed in facial appearance as in mood'.

116 (3.4.146–8) *Nay . . . bridal*: 'No, we must not mistake men for gods, nor expect them to remain as considerate as is appropriate on a wedding-day.'

117 (3.4.151–2) *But now . . . falsely*: 'but now I find I was guilty of corrupting the witness (myself), and he is falsely charged'. (She presumably means that her mood had deflected her from wifely loyalty.)

118 (3.4.193–4) *BIANCA . . . you not*. These words are absent from Q1 but present in F1.

119 (4.1.17) *They . . . not*: (a) 'very often women are thought to retain their honour when they have lost it'; (b) 'very often women retain their honour when they are thought to have lost it'.

120 (4.1.21–2) *As doth . . . all*: Proverbially, 'the croaking raven bodes misfortune'.

121 (4.1.26–8) *having . . . supplied them*: 'having, by their own pressing importunity, overcome the woman, or having gratified the infatuation of some willing mistress,'.

122 (4.1.35–6) *We say . . . belie her*: 'We say "lie on her" [as in "lying on a theme"] when people "belie her" [i.e."tell falsehoods about her"].'

123 (4.1.38–9) *First . . . confess*: Othello refers to the practice of torturing a captive by temporary hanging in order to elicit a confession.

124 (4.1.39–41) *Nature . . . instruction*: 'My body would not, by its trembling, so imitate passion without some good reason.' (He is experiencing the onset of an epileptic fit, but he takes his trembling to be evidence of Desdemona's guilt.)

125 (4.1.37–43) *To confess . . . devil!*: These lines are absent from Q1 but present in F1.

126 (4.1.72–3) *No . . . shall be*: 'No, I would rather know the truth, and, knowing then that I am a cuckold, I also know

what she will be [– either a whore or a victim of my retribution].'

127 (4.1.119) *Do . . . triumph?*:   Cassio is called 'Roman' because Othello associates Romans with triumphal ceremonies and with conquests. Julius Caesar is reported to have said 'Veni, vidi, vici' ('I came, I saw, I conquered').

128 (4.1.120) *What, a customer?*:   F1 has 'What? A customer;'. Q1 lacks these words. A 'customer' is a prostitute.

129 (4.1.127) *Have . . . well*:   Q1 has: 'Ha you stor'd me well'; F1 has: 'Haue you scoar'd me? Well.' Q1's 'stor'd' ('stored') could mean 'produced offspring', but that fits far less well than F1's 'scoar'd', i.e. 'scored', meaning 'slashed, wounded'.

130 (4.1.170–72) *IAGO . . . whore*:   This speech is absent from Q1 but present in F1.

131 (4.1.190–91) *Iago! O Iago . . . Iago!*:   Q1 has: '*Iago*, the pitty.'; F1 has: '*Iago*: oh *Iago*, the pitty of it *Iago*.'.

132 (4.1.265–7) *I may . . . were!*:   'It is not for me to utter criticism. I wish to heaven that he were once again what he could be ("the noble Moor"), if at present he is not what he could be.' However, these lines are ambiguously punctuated in the early texts. Q1 has: 'I may not breathe my censure, / What he might be, if as he might, he is not, / I would to heauen he were.' F1 has: 'I may not breath my censure. / What he might be: if what he might, he is not, / I would to heauen he were.' Interpretations vary widely. Another gloss, based on the Q1 punctuation, might be: 'It is not for me to utter my criticism by suggesting that he may be mad; if he is not what I take him to be, I wish to heaven that he were so.'

133 (4.2.15–16) *head . . . curse*:   In Genesis 3:14–15, God curses the serpent so that it must creep on its belly and eat dust, and Eve's offspring will 'breake [its] head'.

134 (4.2.20–22) *She says . . . secrets*:   'She says enough to sound plausible; yet she would be a naïve procuress if she could not say as much as that. This person is a cunning whore who conceals (like the lock and key of a private room or a cabinet) wicked secrets;'. The person mentioned in the latter sentence could be either Emilia or Desdemona, but the contrast between the bawd and the whore, combined with the

statement that Othello has seen her pray, makes Desdemona more likely: see lines 91–4.

135 (4.2.56) *slow-removing . . . at!*:   Q1 has 'slow vnmouing fingers at'; F1 has 'slow, and mouing finger at'. 'Slow unmoving' seems contradictory; 'slow and moving' seems tautological; hence my emendation. (The idea is that once a person becomes the object of general scorn, the opprobrium is slow to depart.)

136 (4.2.60–63) *The fountain . . . gender in!*:   The imagery derives partly from Proverbs 5:15–18: 'Drinke the water of thy cisterne . . . Let thy fountaine be blessed, and reioyce with the wife of thy youth'; and partly from the traditional homily entitled 'Sermon against Whoredome and Uncleannesse', which describes whoredom as 'that most filthie lake, foul puddle, and stinking sinke, whereunto all kindes of sins and evils flowe' (*Certayne Sermons*, 1569).

137 (4.2.63–5) *Turn . . . hell!*:   This is a famous crux. Different editors interpret the early texts in different ways. Q1 has: 'turne thy complexion there, / Patience thy young and rose-lip'd Cherubin, / I here looke grim as Hell.'; F1 has: 'Turne thy complexion there. / Patience, thou young and Rose-lip'd Cherubin, / I heere looke grim as hell.' The texts may be corrupt. My version means: 'Patience – you who are a young and pink-lipped angel – turn your face to look at Desdemona (yes – look there!), and then you should be so shocked as to renounce your patient demeanour and to look as cruel as a devil from hell.'

138 (4.2.67–8) *as summer . . . blowing*:   'as summer flies are in a slaughter-house: they seem to emerge immediately from the deposited flies'-eggs'. (In other words, 'You are no more honourable than are these disgusting insects associated with impregnated meat and rapid procreation.') EH, p. 277, takes 'with blowing' to mean 'with the blowing of the wind' (matching line 80).

139 (4.2.68–70) *O thou . . . thee*:   'Weed' here may mean either 'weed with the deceptive appearance of a flower' or (since 'weed' could also denote 'any herb or small plant') 'flower'. Shakespeare's Sonnet 94, which concludes with 'Lilies that

fester smell far worse than weeds', suggests that the former
option is preferable. Q1 has: 'O thou blacke weede, why art
so louely faire? / Thou smell'st so sweete, that the sense akes at
thee,'. F1 has: 'Oh thou weed: / Who art so louely faire, and
smell'st so sweete, / That the Sense akes at thee,'.

140   (4.2.75–8) *Committed . . . committed?*:   These lines are absent
from Q1 but present in F1. 'Committed' could mean 'committed adultery', as in 'commit not with man's sworn spouse'
(*King Lear*, Act 3, scene 4).

141   (4.2.80–81) *The bawdy . . . earth*:   The wind is 'bawdy'
because it is free to go anywhere: 'The winde bloweth where
it listeth' (John 3:8). The 'hollow mine of earth' is the
subterranean cavern in which (according to Virgil's *Aeneid*,
Book 1) Aeolus, the wind-god, confines the winds.

142   (4.2.103) DESDEM. *Who . . . lady*:   This line is absent from Q1
but present in F1.

143   (4.2.110–11) *that he . . . misuse?*:   'that he could cast the
slightest aspersion on me, my faults being so minimal?'.

144   (4.2.153–66) *Here . . . make me*:   This passage is absent from
Q1 but present in F1.

145   (4.2.187) *With . . . truth*:   These words are absent from Q1
but present in F1.

146   (4.3.30–52) *I have . . . next*:   These lines are absent from Q1
but present in F1. The willow tree, or a garland made from its
withies, was the emblem of a forsaken and mourning lover
(e.g. of Ophelia in *Hamlet*, Act 4, scene 7).

147   (4.3.54–6) *I called . . . men*:   These lines are absent from Q1
but present in F1.

148   (4.3.59–62) *I have . . . question*:   Again, these lines are absent
from Q1 but present in F1.

149   (4.3.64) *by this heavenly light!*:   (a) 'by this moon above'
(perhaps supposedly visible through a window); (b) 'by this
God-given life of mine'. Emilia then wilfully takes 'by' to
mean not 'in the name of' but 'with the aid of'.

150   (4.3.87–8) *Say . . . laps*:   (b) 'Suppose that they neglect their
responsibilities to us, and squander on outsiders the wealth
that is ours'; (b) 'Suppose that they neglect their marital duties,

and (like Zeus descending as a shower of gold to impregnate Danaë) expend their semen in the vaginas of other women'. Senses (a) and (b) combine in these lines.

151 (4.3.91) *Or scant . . . despite*: 'or, out of spite, reduce whatever they have hitherto allowed us'.

152 (4.3.86–103) *But I . . . us so*: These lines are absent from Q1 but present in F1.

153 (5.1.81–2) *IAGO . . . hence!*: These words are absent from Q1 but present in F1.

154 (5.2.1–3) *It is . . . cause*: Here, 'the cause' appears to mean 'the sin which I am bound to avenge': the sin being (as line 2 makes clear) adultery, which Othello is reluctant to name. The stars are 'chaste', partly because the term 'stars' could include such planets as the moon (associated with chastity, and termed by Shakespeare the 'chaste mistress' and 'watery star'), and partly because they include the constellation Virgo. Furthermore, stars may seem virginally white and aloof. (Conversely, *King Lear*, Act 1, scene 2, suggests that a 'goatish' or lecherous disposition may be blamed on a star.)

155 (5.2.7) *Put . . . light*: 'I must extinguish the light of the candle, and then extinguish the light of Desdemona's life.'

156 (5.2.10–13) *but once . . . relume*. 'Thou cunning'st pattern of excelling nature' means 'you, the most skilful design of Nature when she excels herself'. 'Promethean heat / That can thy light relume' refers to the myth of Prometheus recounted in Hesiod's *Works and Days*: when Zeus marred the world by depriving human beings of fire, Prometheus stole fire from heaven to help them. (Another myth, mentioned in Ovid's *Metamorphoses*, Book 1, is that Prometheus created the human race by imparting life to earth.)

157 (5.2.17) *Justice . . . sword!*: Astræa, the goddess of justice, traditionally bears a set of scales and a sword.

158 (5.2.21–2) *But . . . love*: His tears are 'cruel' because, though they are signs of sorrow, they stem from an implacable avenger. Sorrow which 'strikes where it doth love' perhaps echoes Proverbs 3:12: 'For the Lord correcteth him, whome he loueth . . . '.

159 (5.2.33) *I would . . . soul*:   The idea is that if her spirit is prepared for death by sincere penitence for sins, she will be granted salvation by God.

160 (5.2.41–2) *They . . . diest*:   She means that her only sins are those of loving him too greatly, it being a sin to love a human being more than God. He seems to take her to mean: 'My sins are acts of adulterous love with which I have been burdened during my marriage to you.'

161 (5.2.64) *thou . . . heart*:   F1 has 'my heart'; Q1 has 'thy heart'. F1's version means: 'You turn my heart to stone.' Q1's means: 'You are obdurately impenitent.'

162 (5.2.77) *Alas . . . undone!*:   She means: 'Alas! He is treacherously killed, and I am doomed!'; but Othello takes her to mean: 'Alas! His sin has been discovered, and I am revealed to be an adulteress!'

163 (5.2.83) *Being . . . pause*:   These words are absent from Q1 but present in F1.

164 (5.2. S.D.) *He smothers her*:   Q1 has: '*he stifles her*'; F1 has: '*Smothers her*'. 'Stifles' could mean 'throttles'; 'Smothers' suggests 'suffocates'. (Actors use various means, ranging from bare hands to a pillow or other bedding.) In Q1, the stage-direction is immediately followed by 'O Lord, Lord, Lord' uttered by Desdemona: perhaps she is attempting a prayer to God or is beseeching Othello. (Here, as my emendation, those words precede the S.D.) In F1, that utterance of hers is absent.

165 (5.2.100–2) *Methinks . . . alteration*:   There was an ancient belief that earthquakes were produced by eclipses of the sun and moon. Matthew 27: 45, 51–2, says that as Christ died, there was darkness over all the land for three hours, and 'the earth did quake, and the stones were clouen, / And the graues did open them selues'.

166 (5.2.123–5) *A guiltless . . . farewell!*:   H. H. Furness's Variorum edition of *Othello* quotes a Dr. William Hunt, who claimed that it was entirely plausible for Desdemona to be able to speak briefly at this point, given that 'she died of fracture of the cricoid cartilege of the larynx'. A possible source-tale,

Matteo Bandello's story of the jealous Albanian captain, says that the Albanian's virtuous wife, though mortally wounded by him, regained consciousness for a while and, 'not being willing to let anyone speak ill of him', accused 'nobody but her own misfortune'.

167 (5.2.152–5) *O mistress . . . Iago*:   These lines are absent from Q1 but present in F1.

168 (5.2.186–94) *My mistress . . . villainy!*:   These lines are absent from Q1 but present in F1.

169 (5.2.207) *Shore . . . twain*:   'severed the thread of his life'. (Atropos, one of the three classical Fates, was said to sever with her shears the thread which represented a person's life.)

170 (5.2.220) *as liberal . . . north*:   'as freely as the north wind noisily blows'. Q1 has 'liberall as the ayre'; F1 has 'liberall as the North'.

171 (5.2.246–8) *What . . . willow.'*:   These lines are absent from Q1 but present in F1.

172 (5.2.266–72) *Be not . . . wench*:   These lines, present in F1, are absent from Q1, in which the abrupt shift (from 'tis not so now,' to 'Pale as thy smocke') indicates crude cutting.

173 (5.2.275–6) *Cold . . . chastity*:   Chastity was proverbially likened to ice or snow: 'Be thou as chaste as ice, as pure as snow, thou shalt not escape calumny', says Hamlet to Ophelia.

174 (5.2.285) *that's a fable*:   the 'fable' or superstitious belief that the devil has cloven hooves or feet.

175 (5.2.346) *the base Indian*:   Q1 has 'the base *Indian*'; F1 has 'the base Iudean' (i.e. Judean). F2, however, reverts to 'Indian'. It was sometimes claimed that 'Indians' (whether inhabitants of India or America) were unaware of the value of precious objects in their domains. (Pliny's *Historia Naturalis*, Book 34, Chap. 17, mentions Indians who seem to undervalue pearls; and Michael Drayton's poem *Matilda* says: 'The wretched *Indian* spurns the golden Ore.') Some editors prefer 'Judean', and make various nominations. One is Judas Iscariot, who betrayed Jesus and committed suicide. (He was Judean, whereas the other disciples were Galilean.) Another is King

Herod of Judea, who jealously murdered his wife, Mariamne, thinking her adulterous. Yet another is Jephthah, the warrior who sacrificed his daughter. Bandello's tale of the Albanian captain who killed his virtuous wife compares the captain to Judas. The Bible likens the kingdom of heaven to a pearl; and, in committing suicide, Othello will (according to traditional Christian orthodoxy) be committing a mortal sin which earns damnation.

176 (5.2.349–50) *Drops tears . . . gum*: I preserve the un-grammatical but pleasantly alliterative 'Drops' of Q1 and F1. The Arabian trees may be myrrh trees (Commiphora), which yield aromatic transparent gum. Ovid's *Metamorphoses*, Book 10, says that the Myrrha, a penitent sinner, was changed into a myrrh tree which wept constantly.

177 (5.2.351–5) *And say . . . thus!*: Aleppo, a Syrian city, was an important centre of international trade (and the destination of the master of the ship *Tiger* in *Macbeth*). The Turk is turbaned, being a Muslim; and circumcision was and is a religious rite for Muslims.

178 (5.2.360) *Spartan dog*: 'a kind of bloodhound' (*O.E.D.*). Spartan hunting-dogs, which pursued bears, were renowned: see *A Midsummer Night's Dream*, Act 4, scene 1.

GLOSSARY

Where a pun or an ambiguity is apparent, the meanings are distinguished as (a) and (b), or (a), (b) and (c), etc. Otherwise, alternative meanings are distinguished as (i) and (ii), or as (i), (ii) and (iii), etc. Abbreviations include the following: adj., adjective; adv., adverb; fig., figurative; *O.E.D.*, *Oxford English Dictionary*; vb., verb.

abhor: 4.2.164: disgust.

ability: capacity or power to act.

abode: 4.2.224: sojourn.

abroad: 1.3.382: widely, commonly.

abuse: (i: 1.1.172, 1.2.74, 1.3.60, 390:) corrupt, seduce; (ii: 2.1.227:) degrade, demean; (iii: 2.1.297, 5.1.122) slander; (iv: 3.3.203, 270, 339, 4.2.14, 141, 4.3.61:) deceive.

abuser: 1.2.78: (a) deceiver; (b) corrupter.

accent: 1.1.75: tone of voice.

accident: occurrence, event; **of accident**: 4.1.262: fortuitous.

accommodation: 1.3.238: suitable provision.

achieve: 2.1.61: win.

acknow: **be not acknown**: 3.3.322: reveal no knowledge.

act: 1.1.62, 3.3.331: action.

addiction: 2.2.6: inclination.

addition: (i: 3.4.192:) distinction; (ii: 4.1.104:) title; (iii: 4.2.165:) epithet.

advantage: opportunity; **in the best advantage**: as opportunity best serves; **to th'advantage**: opportunely.

advised: **be advised**: take care.

affect (noun): 1.3.263: desire.

affect (vb.): 3.3.232: desire.

affection: inclination.

affined: bound, constrained.

against: 2.3.355: when exposed to.

agnize: acknowledge.

aim: 1.3.6: guess, surmise.

alarum: 2.3.23: summons, incitement.

allowance: (i: 1.1.126:) approval; (ii: 2.1.49:) reputation.

allowed: approved.

all's one: it's all the same; it doesn't matter.

Almain: German.

almost: **not almost**: 3.3.67: hardly.

amazed: dumbfounded.

an (as conjunction): if; **and if**: 3.4.82: even if.

ancient: ensign (officer of lowest rank), roughly equivalent to regimental sergeant-major.

and-a: verbal padding to sustain a ballad's metre.

answerable: corresponding.

Anthropophagi: cannibals.

antre: cavern.

apprehend: arrest.

apprehension: 3.3.144: idea.

approve: (i: 1.3.11, 2.3.55, 4.3.51:) endorse; (ii: 2.1.44, 4.3.18:) esteem; (iii: 2.3.198, 295:) prove.

approved (adj,): 1.3.77, 2.1.49: esteemed.

apt: (i: 2.1.171:) prompt, ready; (ii: 2.1.278, 5.2.178:) congruous, likely; (iii: 2.3.302:) willing.

arrivance: arrival, landings.

article: item.

arts inhibited: prohibited (magical) practices.

asleep: 4.2.99: stunned, numb.

aspic: asp.

assay (noun): 1.3.18: test.

assay (vb.): 2.3.194: attempt.

atone: reconcile.

attach: arrest.

attend: await.

auld: old.

avaunt: go away.

balance: 1.3.326: set of scales.

battle: 1.1.23: (a) army; (b) battalion.

bauble: 4.1.134: (a) plaything; (b) foolish person.

bawd: procuress.

Bear: 2.1.14: Little Bear (Ursa Minor).

bear (vb.): 1.3.23: overcome; **bear...out**: survive; **bear up to**: sail towards.

beast with two backs (fig.): copulating couple.

beer: **chronicle small beer**: gossip about trivialities.

Before me!: Upon my soul!

beguile: (i: 1.3.66, 210:) rob (usually by trickery); (ii: 2.1.122:) disguise; **beguile her of**: artfully elicit from her.

belch: 3.4.104: vomit.

be-lee'd: intercepted (the wind having been taken from one's sails).

belie: calumniate.

beshrew: (i: 3.4.148) upbraid; (ii: 4.2.130, 4.3.78:) curse.

besort (noun): company.

betray: (i: 5.2.6: a) prove false to; (b) entrap; (ii. 5.2.77: a) entrap; (b) unmask.

bewhore: call a whore.

birlady: by Our Lady (St. Mary).

black: 2.1.131, 132: (a) dark-complexioned; (b) dark-haired; (c) wicked.

blackness: 2.1.133: (a) dark skin; (b) pubis; (c) vagina.

blank: white disc in the centre of an archery target; (hence:) centre.

blazoning: eulogising.

blood: (i: 1.1.168:) consanguinity; (ii: 1.3.104, 123, 327, 333, 2.1.221, 2.3.192, 4.1.270:) natural impulses, passion.

blowing: depositing of flies' eggs.

blown: 3.3.185: (a) inflated; (b) fly-blown.

bob: obtain fraudulently.

boding: ominous.

bolster: 3.3.402: (a) copulate; (b) lie together on a bolster.

bombast (adj.): 1.1.13: padded, turgid.

bookish: erudite but impractical.

boon: favour.

bootless: fruitless, unprofitable.

bound: 1.3.182, 3.1.56, 3.3.216: obliged.

brace: (i: 1.3.24:) state of defence; (ii: 2.3.26:) pair.

brave (vb.): defy.

bravery: bravado.

breeding: 1.3.239: upbringing.

bring in: (i: 3.1.51:) establish; (ii: 3.3.75:) restore.

brow: **brow of the sea**: sea-edge, shore.

bulk: 'framework projecting from the front of a shop; a stall' (*O.E.D.*).

bumper: drinking-vessel filled to the brim.

burning: 2.1.14, 3.3.466: shining.

but: 3.4.117, 5.2.83: simply, only.

butt: end, boundary.

by: 1.3.17: concerning.

cable: 1.2.17: scope.

caitiff: wretch.

callet: low whore.

calmed: 1.1.30: becalmed, (hence:) frustrated.

canakin: small drinking-can.

capable: 3.3.462: comprehensive, capacious.

carack: galleon; **land carack**: 'treasure vessel ashore': heiress, estimable woman.

carry't: get away with it.

carve: strike with a sword.

cashiered: summarily dismissed.

cast: 1.1.148, 2.3.14, 259, 5.2.326: discard, dismiss.

cause: 5.2.1, 3: (a) occasion of revenge, in this case adultery; (b: legal term:) offence with which one is charged.

censure: (i: 2.3.180, 4.1.265:) judgement, opinion; (ii: 5.2.367:) judicial sentence.

certes: assuredly.

chair: 5.1.81, 95, 97: (probably) chair or litter on two poles, carried by two men.

challenge: 1.3.188, 2.1.207: claim.

chamberer: 'one who frequents ladies' chambers; a gallant' (*O.E.D.*).

change: 1.3.315, 347, 2.1.154, 4.3.97: exchange.

charm (noun): magic spell.

charmer: enchantress.

charm your tongue: be silent.

charter: 1.3.245: official privilege.

check: (i: 1.1.147. 3.3.68, 4.3.19:) rebuke; (ii: 2.3.312:) stop.

cherubin (plural regarded as singular): cherub, angel.

chide: 4.2.169: quarrel.

chrysolite: 5.2.145: name of various gems; here probably the topaz.

chuck (term of endearment): darling.

circumscription: restriction.

circumstance: (i: 1.1.13:) long-winded tale; (ii: 3.3.16:) accident, contingency; (iii: 3.3.357:) ceremony; (iv: 3.3.409:) evidence.

circumstanced: governed by circumstances.

cistern: 4.2.62: (a) well; (b) water-tank; (c) pond.

civil: 2.1.233, 2.3.177: well-mannered, urbane; 4.1.64: (a) urbane; (b) urban.

climate, clime: region, country.

clip (vb.): embrace, enfold.

clog: block of wood tied to someone to prevent an escape.

close (adj.): secret, reserved.

closet (adj.): (a) of a private cabinet; (b) of a private room.

clyster-pipe: tube for injecting an enema.

coat: 5.1.25: (a) coat of tough material, e.g. leather; (b) coat with protective lining.

cogging: cheating.

colly (vb.): darken.

coloquintida: colocynth or 'bitter apple', which yielded a bitter purgative medicine.

commission: mandate.

common: open to all.

commoner: 4.2.75: prostitute.

compass: 3.4.70: annual revolution.

complexion: 4.2.63: countenance, face.

compliment: 1.1.63: (a) complement; (b) obsequiousness.

comply with: act in accordance with.

composition: congruity, consistency.

compt: **at compt**: at the day of reckoning, i.e. Doomsday.

compulsive: 3.3.457: (a) compelled; (b) compelling.

conceit (noun): idea, fancy.

conceit (vb.): imagine, speculate.

conception: (i: 3.4.154:) fancy; (ii: 5.2.56:) purpose, design.

condition: disposition.

confine (noun): confinement, restriction.

conjunctive: united, confederate.

conjuration: incantation to exert control.

conjúre: (i: 1.3.105:) influence by magic; (ii: 3.3.297:) adjure.

conscionable: conscientious, scrupulous.

conserved: preserved as a concentrate.

conster: construe, interpret.

consul: senator.

content: 3.1.1: remunerate;
content you: 1.1.41: don't
worry, be assured.
continuate: uninterrupted.
convenience: 2.1.226:
compatibility.
conveniency: 4.2.179:
opportunity.
conversation: 3.3.267: behaviour.
converse (noun): conversation.
conveyance: escort.
convince: 4.1.28: overcome.
cope: 4.1.86: copulate with.
corrigible: corrective.
couch (vb.): recline amorously.
counter-caster: book-keeper,
accountant.
counterfeit: deception.
courser: swift horse.
court of guard: guard-room.
courtship: 2.1.168: courtesy.
cousin: kinsman.
covered with: sexually
penetrated by.
coxcomb: fool.
cozening: cheating, deceiving.
credit: (i: 1.3.2, 2.1.278:)
credibility; (ii: 1.3.97:)
reputation.
critical: censorious.
crusado: Portuguese gold coin
marked with a cross.
cry (noun): (i: 2.3.344) yelping
pack of hounds; (ii: 4.1.124:)
report, rumour.
cry (vb.): 1.3.276: call for,
demand; cry mercy: beg
pardon; cry on: call out,
exclaim.
cuckold: man whose wife
commits adultery.

cunning: in cunning:
knowingly.
cure: stand in bold cure: are in
a healthy state.
curlèd: with curled hair.
customer: 4.1.120: one who
invites custom, (hence:)
prostitute.
daw: jackdaw.
dear: (i: 1.3.85:) zealous;
(ii: 1.3.259:) dire;
(iii: 2.1.282:) loving.
debitor-and-creditor: book-
keeper, office-worker.
defeat: (i: 1.3.338:) disguise;
(ii: 4.2.162:) destroy.
defend: Heaven defend: God
forbid.
delicate: 1.3.351: pleasant.
delighted: delightful.
deliver: (i: 1.3.90, 2.3.206:) relate;
(ii: 1.3.367:) bring to birth.
demerit: merit.
demonstrable: evident,
apparent.
denotement: indication.
Desdemona: (the name means:)
'Ill-fated female'.
desert: uninhabited region (not
necessarily arid).
deserve: 1.1.182: requite.
designment: design, project.
despite: 4.2.118: insult; in
despite: out of spite.
determinate: decisive.
device: trick.
diablo: (Spanish for) devil.
dial: clock.
Dian: Diana, goddess of
chastity.
diet (vb.): feed.

dilate: relate at length.

dilation: 3.3.127: (a) delay, hesitation; (b) pressure; (c) accusation.

direct (adj.): 1.2.86: (a) prompt; (b) appropriate.

directly: (i: 2.1.214:) obviously; (ii: 2.3.330, 3.3.410, 4.2.209:) straightforwardly.

direful: dreadful.

discontented: 5.2.313: expressive of discontent.

discourse: **discourse of thought**: process of thought, meditation.

discover: reveal.

discretion: **do your discretion**: act as you think fit.

dislike: 2.3.40: displease.

disport (noun): physical pleasure.

dispose: **smooth dispose**: urbanely ingratiating manner.

disposition: 1.3.236: arrangement.

disproportioned: inconsistent.

distaste (vb.): disgust.

distempering draughts: intoxicating drinks.

distinctly: 3.3.238: specifically.

distract . . . with: 1.3.323: divide . . . among.

distracted: 2.3.243: alarmed, frightened;

division: 1.1.23: arrangement.

doff: put off.

door: **speak within door**: speak quietly or discreetly.

dotage: infatuation.

dote: talk or act foolishly.

double: **as double as**: twice as strong as.

doubt (noun): fear, apprehension.

doubt (vb.): fear, suspect.

draw with you: share your predicament.

dressed: 5.1.123: have wounds treated; **dress in**: 1.3.26: equip with.

drowsy: soporific.

due course: direct course.

dull: (i: 1.1.122:) drowsy; (ii: 2.1.221:) sluggish, unresponsive.

duty: 1.1.50: respect; **do my duties**: 3.2.2: pay my respects.

ecstasy: 'applied . . . to all morbid states characterized by unconsciousness, as swoon, trance, catalepsy, etc.' (*O.E.D.*).

effect: 1.3.225: result.

else: 2.3.48: besides.

embarked: 1.1.148: engaged, committed.

encave: conceal.

enchafèd: enraged.

endue: induce.

engine: (i: 3.3.358:) cannon; (ii: 4.2.217:) a) plot; (b) device for killing or torturing.

englut: swallow up.

entertainment: 3.3.253: reinstatement.

enwheel: encircle.

epithet: term.

equinox: **just equinox**: 2.3.111: exact counterpoise (just as, at the calendrical equinox, day's duration exactly matches night's).

erring: 1.3.353: errant, roaming.

error: 5.2.110: deviation from the normal course.

estimation: reputation.

eternal: 4.2.132: inveterate, utter.

execution: 3.3.469: operation.

exercise: 3.4.37: religious observance.

exeunt: they go out.

exhibition: financial allowance.

exit: he or she goes out.

expert: experienced.

exsufflicate: inflated, windy.

extincted: extinguished.

extravagant: roaming.

faith: 1.3.294: fidelity.

fall: (i: 3.3.240: a) chance; (b) begin; (ii: 4.1.240:) let fall; **fall in fright**: become alarmed; **fall of swords**: clash of swords on each other.

fame: **wild fame**: extravagant hearsay.

familiar: 2.3.292: amicably complicit

fantasy: 3.3.302: whim, caprice.

fashion: **out of fashion**: incoherently.

fast (adj.): firm, staunch.

fast (adv.): securely.

fathom: 1.1.151: capability.

favour: (i: 1.3.339, 2.1.224, 3.4.123:) face, countenance; (ii: 4.3.20:) charm, attractiveness.

fear (vb.): 1.2.71: terrify:

fearful: alarming.

fell: cruel.

field: (i: 1.1.22, 1.3.85:) battle-field; (ii: 1.3.135:) land in general.

fig: 1.3.319: (a) obscene gesture made by thrusting a thumb between two fingers; (b) familiar term for the disease *Ficus*, piles; (c, possibly) slang term for female labia; **fig's-end**: 2.1.245: (term, with obscene connotations, for:) rubbish.

figure: 1.1.62: design.

find: 2.1.242: recognise.

fineless: boundless.

fitchew: (polecat, hence:) prostitute.

flattery: 4.1.129: self-conceit.

fleer: sneer.

flood: sea.

flood-gate (adj.): torrential.

fluster: make tipsy.

foh!: exclamation of disgust.

folly: (i 2.1.137, 2.1.240: a) foolishness; (b) wantonness; (ii: 5.2.132:) immorality.

fond: (i: 1.3.318, 3.3.448, 4.1.192, 5.2.158:) doting; (ii: 2.1.138:) foolish.

fondly: 3.3.173: dotingly.

footing: landing.

fop (vb.): fool, dupe.

forbear: spare, let alone.

fordo: ruin, destroy.

foregone: previous.

forfend: forbid.

forge (noun): blacksmith's fiery hearth with bellows.

forget: 2.3.175, 228: forget proper behaviour.

forkèd: **forkèd plague**: affliction of cuckoldry.

form: (i: 1.1.50, 2.1.233, 4.2.140:) manner, way, fashion; (ii: 3.3.240, 4.2.157:) physical appearance.

forswear: 4.2.161: renounce, abandon.

fortitude: material strength.

foul: (i: 1.3.65, 117:) wicked; (ii: 2.1.34:) very stormy; (iii: 2.1.140, 141, 142: a:) ugly; (b) wicked.

fountain: 4.2.60: (a) spring; (b) well.

frailty: 4.3.99, 101: susceptibility to temptation.

frank: 3.4.40: (a) liberal, open; (b) unrestrained.

fraught (noun): freight, burden.

free: (i: 1.3.41, 2.3.310, 3.3.188:) willing; (ii: 1.3.265, 394:) generous; (iii: 3.3.258:) guiltless.

freely: unreservedly.

frieze: woollen cloth with a long nap.

from: 1.1.130: contrary to.

front: forehead; **by the front**: by the forelock.

fruitful: bountiful.

fruitfulness: 3.4.34: (a) liberality; (b) amorousness.

full: 2.1.36: perfect.

fulsome: 4.1.36: (a) filthy; (b) nauseating.

function: (i: 2.3.328:) operation of the faculties; (ii: 4.2.27:) trade, business.

fury: 3.4.71: inspired frenzy.

fustian: ranting nonsense.

gall (noun): 4.3.92: the gall-bladder, supposedly the source of rancour and resentment.

gall (vb.): chafe, fret.

galley: low, single-decked vessel, propelled by sails and oars.

game: 2.3.18: sexual sportiveness.

garb: manner (not clothing).

gastness: terror.

gender (noun): sort, kind.

gender (vb.): engender, breed.

generous: high-born, noble.

gentle: 4.1.187-9: (a) well-bred; (b) sweet-natured; (c) pliant, yielding.

german: close relative.

gesture: 4.1.87: attitude.

get: 1.3.191: beget.

gibe (noun): taunt.

go to: (i: 3.4.181:) what nonsense; (ii: 4.2.193:) that's enough; (iii: 4.2.194:) copulate.

God buy, God buy you: God be with you, farewell.

government: (i: 3.3.259: a) management; (b) self-control; (ii: 4.1.231: a) appointment as governor; (b) tenure of office.

gradation: 'the process of advancing step by step' (*O.E.D.*).

grange: country (or farm) house.

gratify: 5.2.214: reward.

green: 2.1.241: inexperienced.

grievance: 1.2.15: infliction.

grim: savage, ruthless.

gripe: grip.

grise: step.

gross: (i: 1.2.72:) palpable, evident; (ii: 3.3.222: a) licentious; (b) flagrant; (iii: 5.2.312:) monstrous.

grossly: 3.3.398: (a) openly;
(b) indecently.

grow: 2.1.190: increase in
number; **grow to waste**: pass
unprofitably.

guardage: 1.2.70: (a)
guardianship; (b) guardian.

guards: 2.1.15: two stars of Ursa
Minor which 'guard' the Pole
Star.

guinea-hen: 1.3.315: (a) bird
with fine plumage; (b) showy
woman; (c, possibly:) whore.

gull: dupe.

guttered: furrowed, gullied.

gyve: fetter.

habit: **thin habits** (fig.):
implausible suggestions.

haggard: adult female hawk
caught wild.

happily: 3.3.241: haply, perhaps.

hard (adv.): hardly; **full hard**:
with extreme difficulty.

hardness: (i: 1.3.233:) hardship;
(ii: 3.4.30:) difficulty.

harlotry: harlot, whore.

harsh: discordant.

haste-post-haste: with the
utmost speed.

haunt about: hang about, loiter
near.

have with you: I'm ready.

having: 4.3.91: possessions,
property.

head: **head and front**: height
and breadth; **make head**:
muster.

heart-strings: 'tendons or
nerves supposed to brace and
sustain the heart' (*O.E.D.*).

hearted: from (or in) the heart.

heat: (i: 1.2.40:) urgency; (ii:
1.3.263:) ardour, eagerness.

heavy: (i: 1.3.258, 4.2.43, 118:)
burdensome, distressing;
(ii: 5.1.42:) sombre.

Hellespont: Dardanelles.

helm: 1.3.272: helmet.

hie: hasten.

high (adv.): 4.2.240: fully.

high-wrought: highly agitated.

hint: (i: 1.3.142:) cue,
opportunity; (ii: 1.3.166:)
suggestion.

hip: **have on the hip**: have an
advantage over.

history: 2.1.251: story.

hobby-horse (fig.): prostitute.

holy writ: the Bible.

home (adv.): 2.1.163: plainly;
put it home: thrust it deeply
in.

honest: (i: 1.1.49, etc.:)
honourable; (ii: 3.3.387:)
virtuous, chaste.

honesty: 5.2.245: moral
integrity.

honour: (i: 1.2.20:) creditable
action; (ii: 2.3.49, 5.2.245:)
reputation; (iii: 4.1.14, 16,
etc.:) chastity; **in honour**: as a
moral duty.

horologe: clock.

hotly: 1.2.44: urgently.

housewife (probably
pronounced '*huzz*-if '):
(i: 1.3.272, 2.1.112:)
housewife; (ii: 4.1.94:) hussy,
shameless woman.

how?: 1.2.93, etc.: what?

humane: 2.1.234: civilised,
courteous.

humour: (i: 3.4.27:) one of the four fluids in the body (blood, phlegm, choler, melancholy) supposed to determine a person's character; (ii: 3.4.123:) disposition, temperament; (iii: 4.2.167:) whim, caprice.

hungerly: hungrily.

Hydra: many-headed snake slain by Hercules.

hyssop: aromatic herb.

ice-brook's temper: (perhaps:) tempered by immersion in water from an icy stream.

idle: (i: 1.2.95, 2.3.255:) trifling; (ii: 1.3.140: a) unprofitable; (b) void of people.

ill-starred: ill-fated.

immediate: 3.3.160: directly touching, personal.

imperious: imperial.

import: concern.

importancy: importance.

imposition: attribution.

imputation: implication.

inclining (adj.): 2.3.320: favourably disposed.

inclining (noun): 1.2.82: side, party.

incontinent: immediately.

incorporate: united in body.

index: prefatory table of contents.

indign: unworthy, shameful.

indirect: 1.3.111: crooked, corrupt.

inference: 3.3.186: implication, imputation.

ingener: inventor.

ingraft (adj.): implanted, habitual.

ingredience: composition of a mixture.

injoint: unite.

innovation: disorder, confusion.

inordinate: immoderate.

insteeped: submerged.

instruction: intimation.

instrument: (i: 4.1.211:) written mandate; (ii: 4.2.46:) instigator.

intentively: intently, attentively.

invention: (i: 2.1.125:) (a) devised topic; (ii: 4.1.185:) imagination.

iterance: repetition.

Janus: Roman god with two faces.

jealous: the meaning ranges between (i) suspicious and (ii) sexually jealous.

jealousy: (i: 3.3.151, etc.:) suspicion; (ii: 3.3.168 on:) sexual jealousy.

jennet: small Spanish horse.

jesses: strips of soft material linking a hawk's legs to the cord from a falconer's wrist.

joint-ring: finger-ring made in two separate parts.

Jove: 2.3.16: Jupiter, the sexually-avaricious supreme deity of the Roman pantheon.

jump (adv.): exactly.

jump (vb.): tally.

just: 1.3.5, 2.3.111: exact.

keep: 3.3.145: conduct; **keep up**: (i: 1.2.59:) sheathe; (ii: 3.1.23:) put away, cease for now.

knave: 1.1.45, 49, 124: servant.

knee-crooking: obsequious.

knot: 4.2.63: entwine in copulation.

'las: alas.

law-day: meeting day for a court of law.

lawn: a fine linen resembling cambric; **measures of lawn**: quantities of fine linen.

lay (noun): 2.3.306: stake in a wager.

lay upon: 2.1.258: give to.

leaden: heavy, depressing.

learn: 1.3.183: teach.

learnèd: 3.3.262: expert.

leet: court of record held by the lord of the manor.

lest: 4.2.37: otherwise.

lethargy: coma.

level with: 1.3.239: match.

liberal (adj.): (i: 2.1.162: a) licentious; (b) outspoken; (ii: 3.4.34, 42: a) generous; (b) licentious.

lie: 3.4.2, 7, 10, 11: (a) dwell, lodge; (b) tell a lie; **lie on**: 4.1.35: (a) calumniate; (b) fornicate with.

lieutenantry: office of lieutenant.

light: 2.3.264: irresponsible.

light of brain: deranged.

line their coats: feather their nests.

lip (vb.): kiss.

list: (i: 2.1.105:) inclination; (ii: 4.1.75:) limit, bounds.

living: 3.3.412: real, valid.

loathly: 3.4.61: (a) in loathing; (b) loathsome.

locust: locust (carob) bean.

look after: 2.1.241: look for, require.

loose: (i: 2.1.235:) immoral; (ii: 3.3.419: a) immoral; (b) indiscreet.

lost: 5.2.269: groundless.

loud: 1.1.149: urgent.

lown: rogue.

lusty: 2.1.286: lustful.

magnifico: title of a Venetian magnate.

maidhood: maidenhood.

main: 2.1.3, 39: open sea.

make: **make after**: go after; **make away**: get away; **what makes he?**: what is he doing?

malignant: 5.2.352: (a) rebellious; (b) malicious.

mammer: (a) hesitate; (b) mumble, stammer; **stand so mamm'ring on**: (a) remain so uncertain; (b) keep on mumbling.

man (vb.): 5.2.270: provide men for, muster.

manage: 2.3.202: maintain.

mandragora: soporific derived from the mandrake plant.

mane: 2.1.13: crest of wave.

marble (adj.): 3.3.463: (probably) resplendent.

mark: **God bless the mark!**: God help me!

marry: by St. Mary.

master: 2.1.205: captain of a ship.

mazard: (originally, drinking cup or bowl; hence, jocularly:) head.

measures of lawn: quantities of fine linen.

meat: 3.3.170, 4.2.172: food, meal.

med'cinable: medicinal.

medicine: 1.3.61, 4.1.45: potion.

mend: **by bad mend**: improve by recognising what is bad.

mercy: **cry mercy**: beg pardon.

mere: 2.2.3: absolute, utter.

mess: 4.1.194: piece, gobbet.

mettle: 4.2.205: (a) spirit; (b) metal.

mince: make light of.

mineral: mineral medicine or poison.

minion: sexual favourite.

minister: 5.2.8: attendant.

miscarry: fail.

mischief: 1.3.204, 205: misfortune.

misuse (noun): misconduct.

mock: **make mocks with**: make a game of.

modern: commonplace.

moe: more.

moraller: moralist.

mortal: deadly, fatal.

mortise: **hold the mortise**: keep any joint intact.

motion: (i: 1.2.75, 1.3.95, 330:) impulse of mind or emotion; (ii: 2.3.161:) action.

mountebank: itinerant quack.

move: (i: 2.3.362, 3.4.15, 164:) plead, supplicate; (ii: 3.3.220, 227, 4.1.229:) perturb, upset.

much: **'tis very much**: it's a grave matter.

mummy: preparation, supposedly having preservative and restorative powers, derived from corpses.

mutiny (vb.): fall to strife.

mutuality: reciprocation.

mystery: profession, business.

naked: 5.2.258: unarmed.

napkin: handkerchief.

native (adj.): natural.

neck: **lay on your neck**: blame you for.

nephew: 1.1.112: (a) descendant; (b) grandson.

new-create: initiate.

next: 1.3.205: (a) surest; (b) quickest.

nice: 3.3.15: slender, thin.

nick: **in the nick**: in the nick of time.

night-gown: dressing-gown.

nonsuit: (cause the withdrawal of a petition:) reject.

north: 5.2.220: the north wind.

nothing (adv.): 2.3.211, 273: not at all.

notorious: 4.2.142, 5.2.239: extreme, exceptional.

object: 5.2.363: spectacle.

observance: observation.

occasion: 2.1.237, 3.1.50: opportunity; **on great occasion**: for an important reason.

ocular: visible, observable.

odd: 2.3.114: fortuitous; **odd-even...o' the night**: (perhaps) around 1 to 2 a.m.

odds: 2.3.172: strife.

off-cap: doff the cap in respect.

offence: 2.3.43, 198: aggression.

officed: on duty

offices: 2.2.8: (probably:) parts of a building which store food and drink, e.g. the kitchen, buttery and cellar.

old: 1.1.37: customary.

open: 1.3.394: guileless.

opinion: (i: 1.3.224:) public opinion; (ii: 2.3.182:) reputation; (iii: 4.2.111:) significance.

opposite: 1.2.67: opposed.

opposition: 2.3.171: combat.

order: ta'en order: made arrangements.

other: 4.2.13: otherwise.

Ottoman (adj.): Turkish.

Ottomites: Turks of the Ottoman Empire.

owe: own.

paddle with: stroke.

paragon (vb.): match in perfection.

parallel (adj.): 2.3.329: in conformity.

parcel: by parcels: piecemeal.

parley: sounds a parley to provocation: utters a summons to a challenger.

parrot: speak parrot: utter words uncomprehendingly.

part: 1.2.31, 1.3.253, 3.3.267: personal quality; in your own part: on your own behalf.

partially: 2.3.205: with undue favour.

particular: 1.3.55: personal, private.

pass (vb.): (i: 1.3.131, 167:) pass through, experience; (ii: 2.3.233:) let pass, disregard.

passage: 5.1.37: people passing by; passage free: free course.

passing (adv.): 1.3.160: exceedingly.

pattern: 5.2.11: model, example.

peculiar: 1.1.60, 3.3.80, 4.1.69: private, personal.

peevish: senseless.

peg: set down the pegs: slacken the strings of a musical instrument; thus, ruin harmony.

perdurable: lasting.

perfect: perfect soul: clear conscience.

period: conclusion.

perplexed: bewildered.

Peter: Saint Peter: gate-keeper of Heaven.

pierce: 1.3.219: penetrate consolingly.

pioner: low-ranking soldier bearing a spade or pickaxe to dig trenches, etc.

pitch (noun): tar.

pith: strength.

place: 1.3.237: lodging.

platform: level place for mounting guns.

play for: 4.3.85: (a) gamble to win; (b) sport amorously to obtain.

pleasance: pleasure, delight.

pliant: suitable.

pluck: pull.

plume up: 1.3.388: (set a crest on: a) complete; (b) fully extend.

ply: solicit.

point on: 5.2.47: point to, presage.

poise: 3.3.83: (a) weight; (b) gravity.

Pole: Pole Star.

policy: prudence.

Pontic Sea: Black Sea.

poppy: 3.3.333: opium, derived from poppies.

portance: bearing, behaviour.

position: 2.1.230: proposition, assertion; **in position distinctly**: categorically.

post–post–haste: with the utmost speed.

potential: 1.2.13: powerful.

potting: boozing.

pottle: half-gallon (2.273-litre) drinking-pot; **pottle-deep**: big as a pottleful.

pox of: curse.

practice: 1.3.102, 3.4.139, 5.2.291: plot, trickery.

practise on or **upon**: plot against, use trickery against.

prank: wanton act.

prate: speak insolently.

precious: 5.2.235: arrant.

prefer: (i: 1.3.109:) put forward, proffer; (ii: 2.1.270:) promote.

preferment: promotion.

pregnant: 2.1.230: cogent, obvious.

preparation: 1.3.14, 221: hostile fleet.

preposterous: extraordinary.

preposterously: extraordinarily, unnaturally.

prerogatived: privileged.

prescription: 1.3.309: (a) immemorial right; (b) medical prescription.

present: immediate.

presently: (i: 2.1.209, 2.3.290:) very soon; (ii: 3.1.36, 5.2.53:) at once.

price: 1.1.11: value, worth.

pride: 3.3.407: sexual desire.

prime: 3.3.406: sexually excited.

prize: 1.2.51: capture, seizure.

probable: 1.2.76: demonstrable.

probal: probable.

probation: proof.

process: proceeding.

proclaim: denounce.

procreant: copulator.

profane: indecent, unseemly.

profit: 3.3.80, 382, 4.2.231: benefit.

Promethean heat: vital warmth, supposedly resembling that of the fire stolen by Prometheus from heaven to help humans.

promulgate: publish.

proper: (i: 1.3.69, 264:) one's own; (ii: 1.3.387, 4.3.34:) handsome.

property: natural character.

Propontic: Sea of Marmora (or Marmara).

propose: 1.1.25: (a) propound a scheme; (b) hold forth in speech.

propriety: proper order.

prospect: view; **to that prospect**: to present themselves thus.

prosperous: favourable.

protest: 4.2.208: affirm.

prove: 4.3.26: become.

provender: fodder: dry food for animals.

public: 4.2.75: common, accessible to all.

pudding: 2.1.247: (perhaps slang for) penis.

puddle: 3.4.141: (make muddy; hence) trouble.

purchase: 2.3.9: acquisition.
pure: 5.2.206: sheer.
put: 5.1.2: thrust; put from: 3.4.86: divert from; put on: 2.1.233, 2.3.331: encourage, incite; put to it: 2.1.118, 3.3.474: force to do; put up: 4.2.181: tolerate.
putting on: incitement.
qualification: 2.1.267: (a) condition; (b) pacification.
qualify: dilute.
quality. (i. 1.3.251, 282: a) character, disposition; (b) profession; (ii: 3.3.356:) attributes.
quarter: in quarter: 2.3.167: in conduct.
quat: pimple or small boil.
quest: 1.2.46: search party.
question: (i: 1.3.23:) military challenge; (ii: 1.3.113:) discourse, conversation.
quicken: (i: 3.3.280:) receive life; (ii: 4.2.68:) give life.
quirk: verbal ingenuity.
quillet: quibble.
raise: 1.1.157, 166, 181, 1.2.29, 43, 2.3.237: arouse.
rack: instrument of torture which stretched the victim and tore his joints.
rank (adj.): lascivious.
rash (adj.): reckless.
rash (adv.): 3.4.78: (a) excitedly; (b) impetuously.
rather: 2.3.220: earlier, sooner.
rebel (vb.): 3.4.39: transgress sexually.
recognizance: solemn token.
recoil: 3.3.239: (a) shrink back in horror; (b) revert.
recommend: 1.3.41: inform.
recover: (i: 2.3.259:) regain favour with; (ii: 5.2.240:) retrieve.
refer me: 1.2.64: appeal.
reference: assignment.
refuse (vb.): 3.1.48: reject.
regard: (i: 1.1.152:) respect, connection; (ii: 2.1.40:) view, prospect.
relume: rekindle.
remembrance: keepsake.
remorse: pity.
repeal: call back.
reprobance: state of reprobacy (utter sinfulness).
reserve: 3.3.298: keep.
resolved: 3.3.183: freed from uncertainty, settled.
respect: (i: 1.3.282:) rank, standing; (ii: 2.1.207, 4.2.192:) regard, favour.
re-stem: head in the opposite direction.
revenge: 4.3.93: vengefulness.
reverend: honoured, respected.
revolt: 3.3.191: (a) treachery; (b) revulsion.
rheum: salt rheum: running cold.
round: 1.3.90: plain, straightforward.
rouse: 2.3.57: (a) bumper, large measure of liquor; (b) carousal, drinking-bout.
rout: 2.3.197: uproar, riot.
ruffian (vb.): 2.1.7: rage.
sadly: 2.1.32: gravely.
Sagittary: inn with the sign of Sagittarius, the centaur.

Saint Peter: gate-keeper of
Heaven.

salt: 2.1.235, 3.3.407: salacious,
lascivious.

sans: without.

satisfy: 5.2.317: (a) placated;
(b) answered.

saucy: insolent.

say: **you have said now**: you
have had your say.

'Sblood: by God's blood.

scan: consider and interpret.

scant: (i: 1.3.267:) neglect;
(ii: 4.3.91:) reduce.

scape: escape.

scattering: random.

scion: 1.3.331: (slip for grafting,
or sucker; hence:) offshoot.

score (noun): (i: 3.4.172, 3:)
twenty; (ii: 3.4.177:) record
of a debt.

score (vb.): 4.1.127: wound.

scurvy (adj.): vile.

scuse: excuse.

sea-bank: sea-shore.

sea-mark: 5.2.268: marked
boundary or limit of
navigable waters.

seamy: 4.2.148: (a) inner;
(b) greasy, dirty.

search: 1.1.157: search-party.

sea-side: sea shore.

sect: (cutting; hence) offspring.

secure (adj.): carefree.

seel, seel up: (originally, to
stitch a hawk's eyelids shut:)
hoodwink, blind.

seeming: 1.3.109, 2.1.234,
3.3.212: external appearance.

segregation: dispersal,
scattering.

self-bounty: personal goodness.

self-charity: love for oneself.

se'nnight: week.

sense: (i: 1.1.130, 1.2.64, 72,
1.3.12, 63, 69, 2.1.71, 3.3.341,
377:) perception, under-
standing; (ii: 4.3.94:) the five
senses; (iii: 5.2.289:) opinion;
to the sense: to the quick.

sentence: (i: 1.3.199, 1.3.216:)
maxim, aphorism; (ii: 1.3.212,
214: a) maxim; (b) judicial
sentence.

sequent: consecutive.

sequester (noun): sequestration,
seclusion.

sequestration: separation.

servitor: servant.

session: sitting of a court of
justice.

set: **double set**: twice twelve
hours; **set on**: instigate; **set
the watch**: mount the guard.

several: separate.

shadowing passion: prefiguring
of passion.

shake off: cast off, abandon.

shame: **for shame**: you should
be ashamed.

shape (vb.): 2.1.55, 3.3.152:
imagine.

shifted away: 4.1.78: contrived
to move away.

shipped: **well shipped**:
provided with a good ship.

shrift: confessional.

sibyl: prophetess.

siege: 1.2.22: (seat of office;
hence:) rank.

sign: (i: 1.1.155:) ensign;
(ii: 1.1.156:) semblance.

signior (from Italian *signore*):
gentleman, sir.

Signiory: governing body of
Venice.

simple: 4.2.20: naïve.

sink: 2.3.196: fall, perish.

sir: play the sir in: act the fine
gentleman when doing.

sirrah (used to address an
inferior): fellow, my man.

sith: since.

skillet: saucepan.

slack (vb.): neglect.

slave: 3.3.445, 4.2.134, etc.:
villain.

slipper (adj.): slippery, shifty.

slubber: sully.

small beer: trivial occupations.

smock: woman's petticoat or
night-dress.

snipe: fool.

snort: snore.

soft you: wait.

solicitor: advocate.

something: 2.3.186: somewhat.

soon at night: towards evening.

sorry: 3.4.47: wretched.

span: 2.3.63: short length: nine
inches.

speak home: speak directly.

speculative: with the power of
sight.

speed: 4.1.108: succeed.

spend: (i: 1.2.48:) utter, say;
(ii: 1.3.209, 2.3.182:) expend,
squander.

spleen: supposed bodily source
of bad temper, impatience,
melancholy and other
feelings; **in spleen**: overcome
by impatience.

splinter (vb.): mend with the
aid of a splint.

spoil: 5.1.54: maim.

spotted with: 3.3.438:
embroidered with.

squire (contemptuous term):
young fellow.

stake: at stake: 4.2.13:
(a) as the item wagered;
(b) at the stake (like a martyr).

stamp (vb.): coin.

stand: stand in an action: be
the object of a law-suit; **stand
in act**: be in progress.

start: 1.1.101: startle, disturb.

startingly: 3.4.78: (a) abruptly,
jumpily; (b) startlingly.

stay: 4.2.172: await.

stead: 1.3.337: help, benefit.

steep-down: precipitous.

still (adv.): constantly.

stillness: 2.3.178: (a) quietness
of behaviour; (b) steadiness.

sting: 1.3.330: (a) goad;
(b) impulse.

stomach: 5.2.76: appetite,
capacity.

stone (noun): 5.2.234:
thunderbolt.

stone (vb.): 5.2.64: turn to
stone, harden.

stop: (i. 2.3.2:) rule of restraint;
(ii: 3.3.124:) check, pause;
(iii: 5.2.264:) power to obstruct.

store: 4.3.84 (a) stock, fill; (b)
populate with their offspring.

stoup: drinking vessel.

straight (adv.): 1.1.136, 1.3.48,
3.3.88, etc.: immediately.

strain: 3.3.253: urge, argue
excessively for.

strangeness: aloofness, estrangement.

stranger: foreigner.

stream: current.

stuff: substance.

subdue: 1.2.81: overpower.

subdued: (i: 1.3.250:) subordinated, submissive; (ii: 5.2.347:) overcome.

substitute: deputy.

subtle: 2.1.236, 4.2.21: crafty, cunning.

success: 3.3.225: sequel, result.

sudden: (i: 2.1.264:) hasty, impetuous; (ii: 4.2.191:) immediate.

sufferance: 2.1.23: suffering of damage or loss.

sufficiency: competence.

sufficient: able.

suggest: 2.3.332: tempt.

supervisor: 3.3.398: (a) looker-on; (b) director.

supply: (i: 3.3.17:) occupy by a substitute; (ii: 4.1.28:) satisfy the desires of.

sustain itself: 5.2.260: find a place, hang.

swag-bellied: pendulous-bellied, big-paunched.

sweeting: darling.

swelling: 2.3.48: proud.

syrup: medicinal decoction.

taint: (i: 1.3.271, 4.2.163:) injure, impair; (ii: 2.1.260:) cast a slur on.

take: **take off**: 5.2.330: take away; **take out**: 3.3.299, 3.4.178, 4.1.147, 150, 152: make a copy of; **take reconciliation**: 3.3.48: accept reconciliation; **take up . . . at the best**: 1.3.173: make the best of.

talk: **you talk**: 4.3.24: you talk pointlessly.

tall ship: tall-masted ship.

taper: candle.

task (vb.): put a strain on, burden.

teem: become pregnant.

tell: (i: 2.2.10:) strike, toll; (ii: 3.3.172:) count; **never tell me**: nonsense.

temper (noun): degree of hardness.

tenderness: youthfulness.

term: **in any just term**: in any respect justly.

terrible: terrifying.

test (noun): 1.3.107: evidence.

theoric: theory.

thing: 3.3.305: (a) pudendum; (b) occurrence.

think upon: 5.2.192: remember.

thrice-driven: winnowed three times: very soft.

tilt: thrust.

time: **in good time**: indeed; **in happy time**: good timing; **keep time**: proceed steadily; **obey the time**: comply with circumstances; **time of scorn**: scornful world.

timorous: terrifying.

tine: wild vetch.

title: 1.2.31: legal right to possession.

toga'd: gowned.

top: 3.3.399, 5.2.136: 'cover', copulate with.

touch: (i: 3.3.82:) test;
(ii: 4.1.193:) concern; **touch
. . . near:** press . . . hard.

toy: (i: 1.3.268:) trifle; (ii:
3.4.154:) idle fancy.

trace for: 2.1.294: (a) keep
hungry for the sake of;
(b) harness to prevent.

trade: occupation, profession.

trance: swoon.

trash: worthless person or stuff.

traverse: march about.

trick: caprice.

trimmed: decked out.

triumph (noun): public
rejoicing.

triumph (vb.): celebrate victory.

trump: trumpet.

truncheon: officer's short staff
(symbol of authority).

tup: 1.1.89: copulate (with a
ewe).

turn (noun): action, deed.

turn (vb.): (i: 4.1.247:) return;
(ii: 4.1.248, 249: a) return; (b)
be unfaithful; (c) turn to men.

twiggen: cased in wicker-work.

Ud's pity: (God's pity:) God
bless us.

unbitted: unbridled.

unblest: (i: 2.3.291:) sinful; (ii:
5.1.34:) wretched.

unbonneted: 1.2.23: (a)
without removing my hat; (b)
having removed my hat.

unbookish: artless, naïve.

undertake: 2.3.311: intercede.

undertaker: be his undertaker:
(a) deal with him; (b,
possibly) arrange his funeral.

undone: 5.2.77: (a) doomed; (b)

revealed to be an adulteress.

unfold: expose, disclose.

unfolding: disclosure,
explanation.

unhandsome: unfair.

unhatched practice: covert
machination.

unkind: 4.1.218: unnatural,
strange.

unlace: undo.

unperfectness: imperfection.

unproper: 4.1.68: (a) not
exclusively one's own;
(b) improper, indecent.

unprovide: disarm.

unquietness: perturbation.

unwitted: deranged.

use (noun): 4.1.269: custom,
habit.

use (vb.): 5.2.71: copulate with.

usurped: false.

vain: useless.

vantage. to th'vantage: in
addition.

vessel: 4.2.85: body.

vexation: 1.1.72: torment.

vicious: 3.3.149: (a) wicked;
(b) mistaken.

violence: (i: 1.3.249:) violation
of convention; (ii: 2.1.217:)
vehemence.

virtue: 1.3.318, 319: (a) power;
(b) moral nature.

virtuous: 3.4.109: efficacious.

visage: 1.1.50: assumed facial
appearance.

voice: 1.3.225, 260: vote,
approval.

voluble: glib.

votarist: person bound by vows
to a religious life.

vouch (noun): testimony.
vouch (vb.): bear witness.
wage: 1.3.30: hazard.
warrant: **out of warrant**:
 illegal.
warranty: authorisation.
wash: drench.
wasted: 1.3.84: (a) past;
 (b, perhaps) squandered.
watch (noun): 2.3.12, 107:
 guard, guard duty.
watch: (i: 2.3.47, 52:) keep
 guard; (ii: 2.3.117, 3.3.288:)
 stay awake; (iii: 3.3.23:)
 prevent a hawk from sleeping
 in order to tame it;
 (iv: 4.2.234:) watch for.
water: **by water**: 4.2.106: (a) by
 way of water; (b) in the form
 of tears.
way: **out of the way**: (i:
 1.3.356:) irrelevant, pointless;
 (ii: 3.4.79:) gone astray,
 missing.
weed: 4.2.68: (a) weed with
 the appearance of a flower;
 (b) any herb or small plant;
 weed up: weed out.
well-painted: well-simulated.
what are you?: who are you?
wheeling: circulating.
whip me such: 1.1.49: gratify
 me by whipping such.
whipster: whippersnapper,
 upstart.
whistle off: release a hawk
 from the fist.

white: 2.1.133: (a) man of light
 complexion; (b) wight, man.
wholesome: 1.1.144: healthy,
 beneficial.
wight: person.
wild fame: extravagant hearsay.
will: (i: 1.3.344. 3.3.235, 239,
 4.2.154:) desire, particularly
 sexual desire; (ii: 1.3.388:)
 purpose.
willow: weeping willow,
 emblem of disappointed love.
wink: close eyes.
wise: 4.1.228: sane.
wit: (variously) wisdom,
 intelligence, cleverness.
witty: 2.1.131: (a) wise;
 (b) clever.
womaned: accompanied by
 a woman.
wrangle: dispute angrily.
wretch: 'a term of playful
 depreciation' (*O.E.D.*).
writ: **holy writ**: the Bible.
wrought: 5.2.344: worked
 upon, moved.
yawn: 5.2.102: gape open.
yerk: stab.
yet: **that I do not yet**: if I do
 not still.
yoked: 4.1.66: (a) bound in
 marriage; (b) yoked like an
 ox.
Zounds: by God's wounds.

WORDSWORTH CLASSICS

REQUESTS FOR INSPECTION COPIES Lecturers wishing to obtain copies of Wordsworth Classics, Wordsworth Poetry Library or Wordsworth Classics of World Literature titles for inspection are invited to contact: Dennis Hart, Wordsworth Editions Ltd, Crib Street, Ware, Herts SG12 9ET; E-mail: dennis.hart@wordsworth-editions.com. Please quote the author, title and ISBN of the books in which you are interested, together with your name, academic address, E-mail address, the course on which the books will be used and the expected enrolment.

Teachers wishing to inspect specific core titles for GCSE or A-level courses are also invited to contact Wordsworth Editions at the above address.

Inspection copies are sent solely at the discretion of Wordsworth Editions Ltd.

JANE AUSTEN
Emma
Mansfield Park
Northanger Abbey
Persuasion
Pride and Prejudice
Sense and Sensibility

ARNOLD BENNETT
Anna of the Five Towns
The Old Wives' Tale

R. D. BLACKMORE
Lorna Doone

M. E. BRADDON
Lady Audley's Secret

ANNE BRONTË
Agnes Grey
The Tenant of Wildfell Hall

CHARLOTTE BRONTË
Jane Eyre
The Professor
Shirley
Villette

EMILY BRONTË
Wuthering Heights

JOHN BUCHAN
Greenmantle
The Island of Sheep
John Macnab
Mr Standfast
The Thirty-Nine Steps
The Three Hostages

SAMUEL BUTLER
Erewhon
The Way of All Flesh

LEWIS CARROLL
Alice in Wonderland

M. CERVANTES
Don Quixote

ANTON CHEKHOV
Selected Stories

G. K. CHESTERTON
The Club of Queer Trades
Father Brown: Selected Stories
The Man Who Was Thursday
The Napoleon of Notting Hill

ERSKINE CHILDERS
The Riddle of the Sands

JOHN CLELAND
Fanny Hill – Memoirs of a Woman of Pleasure

WILKIE COLLINS
The Moonstone
The Woman in White

JOSEPH CONRAD
Almayer's Folly
Heart of Darkness
Lord Jim
Nostromo
Sea Stories
The Secret Agent
Selected Short Stories
Victory

J. FENIMORE COOPER
The Last of the Mohicans

STEPHEN CRANE
The Red Badge of Courage

THOMAS DE QUINCEY
Confessions of an English Opium Eater

DANIEL DEFOE
Moll Flanders
Robinson Crusoe

CHARLES DICKENS
Barnaby Rudge
Bleak House
Christmas Books
David Copperfield
Dombey and Son
Best Ghost Stories
Great Expectations
Hard Times
Little Dorrit
Martin Chuzzlewit
The Mystery of Edwin Drood
Nicholas Nickleby
The Old Curiosity Shop
Oliver Twist
Our Mutual Friend
The Pickwick Papers
Sketches by Boz
A Tale of Two Cities

BENJAMIN DISRAELI
Sybil

FYODOR DOSTOEVSKY
Crime and Punishment
The Idiot

ARTHUR CONAN DOYLE
The Adventures of Sherlock Holmes
The Best of Sherlock Holmes
The Case-Book of Sherlock Holmes
The Hound of the Baskervilles
The Return of Sherlock Holmes
The Lost World & Other Stories
Sir Nigel
A Study in Scarlet & The Sign of The Four
Tales of Unease
The Valley of Fear
The White Company

GEORGE DU MAURIER
Trilby

ALEXANDRE DUMAS
*The Count of
Monte Cristo
The Three Musketeers*

MARIA EDGEWORTH
Castle Rackrent

GEORGE ELIOT
*Adam Bede
Daniel Deronda
Felix Holt the Radical
Middlemarch
The Mill on the Floss
Silas Marner*

HENRY FIELDING
Tom Jones

RONALD FIRBANK
*Valmouth &
Other Stories*

F. SCOTT FITZGERALD
*The Diamond as Big as
the Ritz & Other Stories
The Great Gatsby
Tender is the Night*

GUSTAVE FLAUBERT
Madame Bovary

JOHN GALSWORTHY
*In Chancery
The Man of Property
To Let*

ELIZABETH GASKELL
*Cranford
North and South
Wives and Daughters*

GEORGE GISSING
New Grub Street

OLIVER GOLDSMITH
The Vicar of Wakefield

KENNETH GRAHAME
The Wind in the Willows

G. & W. GROSSMITH
Diary of a Nobody

H. RIDER HAGGARD
She

THOMAS HARDY
*Far from the Madding
Crowd
Jude the Obscure
The Mayor of Casterbridge*

*A Pair of Blue Eyes
The Return of the Native
Selected Short Stories
Tess of the D'Urbervilles
The Trumpet Major
Under the Greenwood
Tree
The Well-Beloved
Wessex Tales
The Woodlanders*

**NATHANIEL
HAWTHORNE**
The Scarlet Letter

O. HENRY
Selected Stories

JAMES HOGG
*The Private Memoirs
and Confessions of a
Justified Sinner*

HOMER
*The Iliad
The Odyssey*

E. W. HORNUNG
*Raffles: The Amateur
Cracksman*

VICTOR HUGO
*The Hunchback of
Notre Dame
Les Misérables*
IN TWO VOLUMES

HENRY JAMES
*The Ambassadors
Daisy Miller &
Other Stories
The Europeans
The Golden Bowl
The Portrait of a Lady
The Turn of the Screw &
The Aspern Papers
What Maisie Knew*

M. R. JAMES
*Ghost Stories
Ghosts and Marvels*

JEROME K. JEROME
Three Men in a Boat

SAMUEL JOHNSON
Rasselas

JAMES JOYCE
*Dubliners
A Portrait of the Artist
as a Young Man*

OMAR KHAYYAM
The Rubaiyat
TRANSLATED BY E. FITZGERALD

RUDYARD KIPLING
*The Best Short Stories
Captains Courageous
Kim
The Man Who
Would Be King
& Other Stories
Plain Tales from
the Hills*

D. H. LAWRENCE
*The Plumed Serpent
The Rainbow
Sons and Lovers
Women in Love*

SHERIDAN LE FANU
*In a Glass Darkly
Madam Crowl's Ghost
& Other Stories*

GASTON LEROUX
The Phantom of the Opera

JACK LONDON
*Call of the Wild &
White Fang*

KATHERINE MANSFIELD
Bliss & Other Stories

GUY DE MAUPASSANT
The Best Short Stories

HERMAN MELVILLE
*Billy Budd & Other
Stories
Moby Dick
Typee*

GEORGE MEREDITH
The Egoist

H. H. MUNRO
*The Collected Stories
of Saki*

**THOMAS LOVE
PEACOCK**
*Headlong Hall &
Nightmare Abbey*

EDGAR ALLAN POE
*Tales of Mystery and
Imagination*

FREDERICK ROLFE
Hadrian VII

SIR WALTER SCOTT
*Ivanhoe
Rob Roy*

WILLIAM SHAKESPEARE
All's Well that Ends Well
Antony and Cleopatra
As You Like It
The Comedy of Errors
Coriolanus
Hamlet
Henry IV Part 1
Henry IV Part 2
Henry V
Julius Caesar
King John
King Lear
Love's Labours Lost
Macbeth
Measure for Measure
The Merchant of Venice
The Merry Wives of Windsor
A Midsummer Night's Dream
Much Ado About Nothing
Othello
Pericles
Richard II
Richard III
Romeo and Juliet
The Taming of the Shrew
The Tempest
Titus Andronicus
Troilus and Cressida
Twelfth Night
Two Gentlemen of Verona
A Winter's Tale

MARY SHELLEY
Frankenstein
The Last Man

TOBIAS SMOLLETT
Humphry Clinker

LAURENCE STERNE
A Sentimental Journey
Tristram Shandy

ROBERT LOUIS STEVENSON
Dr Jekyll and Mr Hyde
The Master of Ballantrae & Weir of Hermiston
Travels with a Donkey & Other Writings

BRAM STOKER
Dracula

HARRIET BEECHER STOWE
Uncle Tom's Cabin

R. S. SURTEES
Mr Sponge's Sporting Tour

JONATHAN SWIFT
Gulliver's Travels

W. M. THACKERAY
Vanity Fair

LEO TOLSTOY
Anna Karenina
War and Peace

ANTHONY TROLLOPE
Barchester Towers
Can You Forgive Her?
Dr Thorne
The Eustace Diamonds
Framley Parsonage
The Last Chronicle of Barset
Phineas Finn
The Small House at Allington
The Warden
The Way We Live Now

IVAN SERGEYEVICH TURGENEV
Fathers and Sons

MARK TWAIN
Tom Sawyer & Huckleberry Finn

JULES VERNE
Around the World in Eighty Days & Five Weeks in a Balloon
Journey to the Centre of the Earth
Twenty Thousand Leagues Under the Sea

VIRGIL
The Aeneid

VOLTAIRE
Candide

LEW WALLACE
Ben Hur

ISAAC WALTON
The Compleat Angler

EDITH WHARTON
The Age of Innocence
Ethan Frome

GILBERT WHITE
The Natural History of Selborne

OSCAR WILDE
De Profundis, The Ballad of Reading Gaol, etc.
Lord Arthur Savile's Crime & Other Stories
The Picture of Dorian Gray
The Plays
IN TWO VOLUMES

VIRGINIA WOOLF
Mrs Dalloway
Orlando
To the Lighthouse
The Waves

P. C. WREN
Beau Geste

CHARLOTTE M. YONGE
The Heir of Redclyffe

TRANSLATED BY VRINDA NABAR & SHANTA TUMKUR
Bhagavadgita

EDITED BY CHRISTINE BAKER
The Book of Classic Horror Stories

SELECTED BY REX COLLINGS
Classic Victorian and Edwardian Ghost Stories

EDITED BY DAVID STUART DAVIES
Shadows of Sherlock Holmes
Selected Stories of the Nineteenth Century